MOONSHINE

THE STORY OF MOONSHINE AND HOW TO MAKE YOUR OWN

CHRISTOPHER G. YORKE

i

Moonshine

By Christopher G. Yorke, M. Ed

Published by:

Mason Creek Publishing

2500 Sunrise Street

Kelso, WA 98626

360-600-9615

cyorke57@gmail.com

Copyright © 2023 by Mason Creek Publishing

Cover Art By Sandra Yorke

ISBN 9798861843256

Printed in the United States of America

Library of Congress CIP Data Pending

DISCLAIMER:

The purpose of this book is to provide distilling education to those who are licensed or are planning to get licensed to legally make distilled spirits. The example pictures used in the book were staged using water - actual spirits were not produced. However, the pictures and processes illustrated are based on actual distilling procedures and are a correct depiction of the process. The information provided is correct and factual. The author and/or Mason Creek Publishing are not responsible for the use or misuse of the information herewithin.

Contents

PREFACE

The purpose of Moonshine book is to provide you with some of the interesting history of moonshine and to teach you how to make high quality moonshine. Everything you need to know is in the book. I have tried to focus on the essential information while avoiding unnecessary topics that waste your time. And you won't need to read a bunch of different books or spend countless hours searching the internet for the information you need - it is ALL here. There are many different approaches to distilling alcohol and making moonshine, some of which are unsafe and even dangerous. This book contains the basic concepts and proven procedures you need in order to successfully make your own moonshine in a safe manner, including clear pictures of every step. Please remember that in order to distill spirits legally you need a license. For a small distiller you can apply for a craft distiller's license. You will need to apply for a Federal license and check with the requirements of your particular State.

1

The Story of Moonshine

Moonshine originated in England, Scotland, and Ireland. In Ireland they made something called Poitin. Also called Poteen and Potcheen, this whiskey was basically Irish moonshine. The name comes from the Irish word "pota" meaning small pot referring to the small copper pot distillers would use. Poitin is made from cereal grains, whey, sugar beets, molasses, or potatoes. Its alcohol content ranges between 40 and 90% abv (80-180 proof). It is illegal to produce. When immigrants came to America from these countries many of them settled in the Appalachian region. They brought their distilling skills with them and used local corn to distill whiskey. The term "moonshine" originated in Europe and was used in England in the 1700's. It originally referred to occupations that required night work. In the late 18th century, the term was used in England to describe illicit or smuggled liquor. This was because the liquor was made and smuggled during the night, by the light of the moon. Moonshine is also known as new make spirit, white whiskey, white dog, and white lightning. In it's most basic form moonshine is a clear, unaged whiskey with a corn base, a high alcohol content, and it is made illegally.

For the first 200 years of its consumption in America it was legal to produce moonshine. However, the United States started taxing liquors and spirits shortly after the American Revolution. In 1791, the federal government passed a distilled spirits tax. The "whiskey tax," as it was called, was proposed by Alexander Hamilton and passed by congress. The tax revenue was needed to pay for the expenses incurred from the war. Needles to say, the American people were not happy with the new tax and many kept on making their own whiskey and ignored the tax. Violence and destruction ensued and the "whiskey rebellion" had begun. Farmers/distillers in western Pennsylvania protested by tarring and feathering tax collectors and attacking their homes. In the early frontier days of American history moonshine wasn't just a hobby, it was a source if income. Many farmers relied on moonshine manufacturing to survive. Low value corn crops could be turned into high value whiskey and paying distilled spirits taxes was not popular. The rebellion was eventually quashed and the whiskey tax remained in place until 1802 when it was finally repealed by the Thomas Jefferson administration.

Making homemade liquor (moonshine) was legal in the United States until Prohibition began during the Harding administration. Prohibition began with the enactment of the 18th Amendment in January, 1920. The amendment prohibited the manufacture, sale, and transport of all intoxicating liquors in the United States. Making moonshine became even more popular after prohibition began. In fact, the Prohibition era is considered the golden age of moonshining. It was pretty simple, people could not buy liquor so they made their own.

The 21st Amendment repealed the 18th Amendment on December 5, 1933 thereby ending Prohibition, but moonshine production continued to boom. The Great Depression continued to bring hardship to many Americans during this time period and many people relied on moonshining to earn money. Although alcohol was legal once again, the profits from illegal moonshining were still attractive. Illegal moonshiners were not licensed and did not pay the required liquor taxes. The Appalachian mountains were where the distilling of moonshine thrived due to its limited road network. Drivers or "runners" knew the roads and could outrun the cops who were trying to find their distilling operations. After Prohibition ended, some of the moonshine runners formed NASCAR with the intent of keeping their driving skills sharp through organized races.

These days, the production and sale of distilled spirits is legal in the United States as long as you have the required license and permits, and pay the required taxes. Without the appropriate licensing it is illegal to produce distilled spirits, even for personal use.

FAMOUS MOONSHINERS

Marvin "Popcorn" Sutton

Marvin "Popcorn" Sutton was an American moonshiner and bootlegger. He was born in Maggie Valley, North Carolina in 1946 and learned to make moonshine from his father. He came from a long line of bootleggers and considered moonshining his birth right. Sutton  was known for being surly, foul-mouthed, and anachronistic. In the 1960s or 1970s, Sutton was given the nickname of "Popcorn" after he attacked a bar's faulty popcorn vending machine with a pool cue.

Sutton died in March 2009 at the age of 62. He was revered as a folk hero and rebel. He is still referred to as the "king of moonshine", although he was certainly not a positive role model.

Robert Glenn "Junior Johnson

Robert Glenn "Junior" Johnson was a moonshine runner and eventually became a NASCAR driver. He was born in Wilkesboro, North Carolina on June 28, 1931. Johnson began making and running moonshine at a young age. Johnson became part owner of Piedmont Distillers in 2007. He introduced Junior Johnson's Midnight Moon, a moonshine based on the Johnson family's recipe. The moonshine is made from corn, crafted in small batches, and triple distilled.

Al Capone

Al Capone ran moonshine during Prohibition. Archaeologists in South Carolina discovered the remains of a 1920s-era moonshine still that may have been part of Al Capone's illegal liquor operation. The still is believed to have belonged to Benjamin Villeponteaux, who ran moonshine with Al Capone.

Enoch Lewis "Nucky" Johnson

Enoch Lewis Johnson was a famous moon-shiner and bootlegger during the Prohibition era. He was a political boss who ran Atlantic City from the 1910s to the 1930s. Johnson began his political career as the Atlantic County sheriff in 1908. He then became the executive secretary of the Republican Party. Johnson died in December 1968.

MAKING YOUR OWN MOONSHINE

Making moonshine can be a safe and rewarding pursuit if the correct procedures are followed. This requires the correct supplies and equipment, and the correct procedures. Also remember that distilling any spirits requires a license. Check with your State for the required licensing.

For the remainder of this book, we will look at the supplies and equipment needed, distillery setup guidelines, the process of cooking mash, fermentation procedures, distilling steps, and bottling.

2

Supplies and Equipment

MOONSHINE STILLS

There are many different types of stills that can be used to make moonshine. Many of the old-time moonshiners, and probably even some today, make there own stills from spare parts and junk they having laying around - I do not advise this practice. I recommend buying a still kit or buying a still that is built and ready to go. A popular type of still for making moonshine, and other spirits, is the copper alembic pot still. They are easy to use, reasonably priced, and make great moonshine. The still featured in this book is a copper pot still. We will refer to it when demonstrating the distilling process later in the book. The still was purchased from Mile High Distilling and is an excellent still. You can see their products at milehidistilling.com.

ALEMBIC POT STILL, PARTS AND SETUP

The copper alembic pot still is the oldest type of still used. Many people, including some commercial distilleries, believe the Alembic Copper Still produces the best tasting whiskey and it works well for making moonshine. It consists of the kettle/boiler, still head, lyne arm, vapor thermometer, condenser, and coiled condenser tubing, (goes down into the condenser). The fermented wash is placed into the still and heated by the burner for distillation. Alcohol vapors accumulate in the still head, travel past the vapor thermometer and into the condenser tubing. As the vapor travels down the condenser tubing into the condenser, the cool water in the condenser converts the vapor back into liquid. The liquefied alcohol exits the condenser through the food-grade condenser discharge tube and goes into a distillate collection jar. All of the examples in this book will relate to using a 8 gallon (30.28 liter) still.

Still Parts

A - Kettle
B - Still head
C - Vapor thermometer
D - Lyne arm
E - Condenser
F - Distillate tube
G - Burner
H - Alcohol parrot
I - Distillate collection
jar

POT, BOILER, KETTLE

The still pot is used to heat the wash during the first distillation, or the low wines during the second distillation, in order to boil the solution and vaporize the alcohols within. Pots come in many sizes from a gallon or so up the thousands of gallons in commercial distilleries.

ONION HEAD

The purpose of the onion head is to collect vapors as the still contents is heated. The vapors make their way up and into the lyne arm. This particular onion head has a vapor thermometer mounted on the side.

VAPOR THERMOMETER

The vapor thermometer indicates the temperature of the distillate vapor during distillation. Keeping track of temperature is a critical part of successful distilling. The thermometer shown is a dial thermometer showing both Fahrenheit and Celsius temperatures. Many stills come with a vapor thermometer already attached.

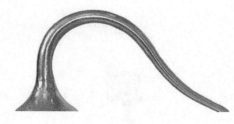

LYNE ARM

The lyne arm goes from the onion head to the condenser. It transports the vapor to the condenser.

WORM CONDENSER

The condenser contains copper tubing that carries alcohol vapor (distillate) from the still. The condenser is full of cold water which cools the vapor and returns it to a liquid state. As the distillate leaves the condenser it will flow into a collection jar.

Alcohol vapor from still

Water outlet

Cold water inlet

Distillate outlet to collection jar

CONDENSER WORM

The condenser worm or tubing carries the vapor from the still through the cold water inside the condenser. This is where it returns to a liquid state. From there it is carried out to the collection jar.

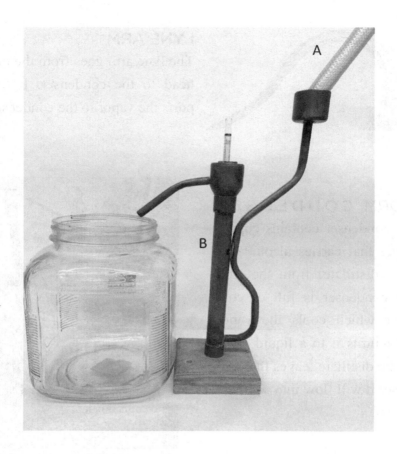

ALCOHOL PARROT
AND DISTILLATE COLLECTION JAR

The alcohol parrot collects distillate from the food grade distillate tube (A). The alcohol hydrometer is placed into the parrot tube (B). Once the distillate has filled the parrot tube, abv can be read off of the hydrometer. See "how to use an alcohol hydrometer" on page 15. Distillate flows out of the parrot and into the collection jar.

DISTILLING WITH A POT STILL

This is just a general description of how to use a pot still to get started with. As you continue reading through the book you will learn the more specific details and processes.

Everything starts with cooking the mash to convert the starches in the grains into fermentable sugars. The liquid in the mash is called the wort. The next step is to ferment the wort for 3 to 5 days. Once the wort is finished fermenting it is called a wash and is removed from the fermentation bucket (fermenter) and placed into the pot still.

The first distillation is called a **stripping run**. The purpose of the stripping run is to simply remove all of the alcohol from the fermented wash. After placing the wash into the still and getting everything set up, a medium heat is applied to the bottom of the still. This can be either an electric burner or a propane burner. After 90 minutes or so, depending on the size of the wash, the first drips will begin coming out of the still. The temperature will slowly rise and the flow of distillate will increase to several drips per second. This rate is maintained for the entire run. As the run continues the temperature will go up and the alcohol by volume (abv) of the distillate will go down. Most distillers stop the run at about 10% abv or when the vapor temperature is 96°C (204.8°F). The collected distillate from this run is called the **low wines**.

The second distillation is called the **spirit run**. This is the run where the different types of alcohol are boiled and turned into vapors at different temperatures. As the still temperature slowly increases, the different alcohols will exit the still, go through the condenser, return to a liquid form, and drip out into a collection jar. This distillate will be separated, or cut, into foreshots, heads, hearts, and tails.

The hearts, and possibly a little of the heads and tails, are what we keep to make moonshine and other spirits from. This process is the basically the same for an alembic pot still and a column still used in pot still mode. We will get much deeper into the process later in the book.

ALCOHOLOMETER
(ALCOHOL HYDROMETER)

The alcoholometer, measures the specific gravity of the distillate. One side of the alcoholometer indicates the abv and the other side shows the proof of your spirit. Specific gravity indicates how dense a liquid is. Alcohol is less dense than water so the hydrometer will sink lower in it compared to water. See below for a complete explanation of how the hydrometer works and how to use it. You can purchase an alcohol hydrometer from brew stores or online for about $12.00.

How to Use an Alcoholometer (Alcohol Hydrometer)

The alcohol hydrometer has two scales, one on each side. One side shows the abv percentage and the other shows the proof. Proof is simply twice the abv. For example, 40% abv is 80 proof.

When you place the hydrometer into a parrot, graduated cylinder, or any other receptacle it will float and you can read the abv or proof. If your reading was as shown with the arrow on the next page, you would have an abv of 45% and a proof of 90.

Each increment on the abv scale is 1.

Each increment on the proof scale is 2.

Be sure to read at the meniscus. The meniscus is the curved upper surface of a liquid in a tube. When you place the hydrometer into the distillate a meniscus will form around it. Make sure you read at the bottom of the meniscus, not at the part that rises up on the side of the hydrometer. The picture on the next page shows how to read the proof on an alcohol hydrometer correctly. In this case the correct reading would be 164 proof.

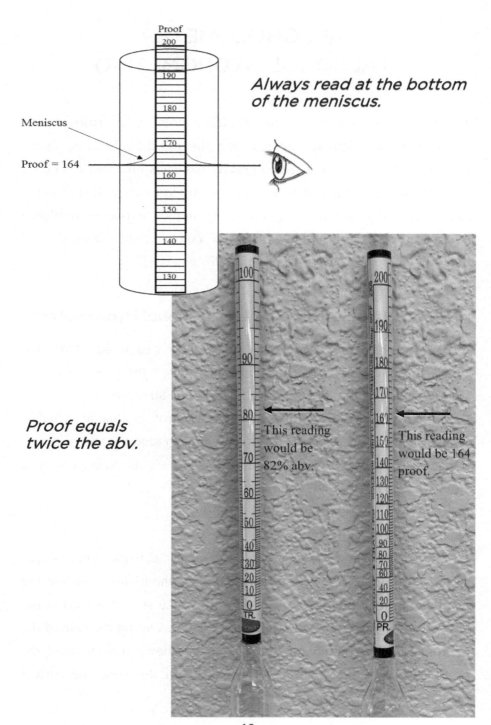

Proof

200

190

180

Meniscus

170

Proof = 164

160

150

140

130

*Always read at the bottom
of the meniscus.*

*Proof equals
twice the abv.*

This reading
would be
82% abv.

This reading
would be 164
proof.

16

Adjusting the abv for Temperatures
Above or Below 15.5ºC (60ºF)

The alcohol hydrometer is calibrated to work at 15.5°C (60°F). If the temperature of your distillate is above or below 15.5°C (60°F) you need to make an adjustment to your reading. As the distillate temperature increases the alcohol becomes less dense, the hydrometer sinks lower into the distillate and you get a false high reading. You need to subtract from the hydrometer reading in order to get the correct abv. As the distillate temperature decreases the alcohol becomes more dense, the hydrometer rises and you get a false low reading. You need to add to the hydrometer reading in order to get the correct abv. The chart on page 18 shows you the amounts to add or subtract at the various distillate temperatures. Make sure you check the <u>distillate temperature</u> and don't use the ambient air temperature when making these adjustments. Check the distillate temperature by inserting your long stem thermometer into your parrot tube.

Subtract from the abv reading when the distillate temperature is above 60°F.

Add to the abv reading when the distillate temperature is below 60°F.

Photocopy the chart on page 18 and post it on the wall next to your still.

ABV TEMPERATURE CORRECTION

Temp ºF	0-25 Proof	25-50 Proof	50-200 Proof
100	-14	-12	-16
95	-12	-10.5	-14
90	-10	-9	-12
85	-8.5	-7.5	-10
80	-7	-6	-8
75	-5	-4.5	-6
70	-3	-3	-4
65	-1.5	-1.5	-2
60	0	0	0
55	+1.5	+1.5	+2
50	+3.5	+3	+4
45	+5	+4.5	+6
40	+7	+6	+8
35	+9	+8	+10
30	+10.5	+9	+12
25	+12	+10.5	+14
20	+14	+12	+16
15	+16	+13.5	+18
10	+18	+15	+20
5	+19	+16.5	+22
0	+21	+18	+24

SACCHAROMETER
(SUGAR HYDROMETER)

A saccharometer is a hydrometer used for determining the amount of sugar in a solution. In the case of making whiskey, the sugar hydrometer is used to measure the **specific gravity (SG)** in the mash, and the wash after fermentation is complete. Once we know the SG of the mash or the wash we can use the chart on page 144 to figure out the sugar content. We use this information to determine the potential alcohol in the mash and the wash. **Potential alcohol (PA)** is an estimate of the percentage of the mash or wash that will become alcohol from fermentation by the yeast. The sugar hydrometer has two scales, a specific gravity scale and a potential alcohol scale. The diagram on the right shows each scale. You can check the SG on the scale and also read the corresponding PA scale. It is more accurate however, to read the SG and use the chart on page 22 or page 141 to identify the PA. When you purchase a sugar hydrometer a small version of the chart comes with it. A saccharometer can be purchased from a brew store or from Amazon.com for about $12.00.

Reading the SG and PA

The more sugar that is in the mash or the wash the higher the SG will be. This means the density of the solution is higher. The higher the SG the higher the hydrometer will float in the solution. This will show a higher SG and PA reading on the hydrometer. As an example, look at the saccharometer on page 20. The correct reading would be 1.070 for SG and 9.20 percent for PA. Again, using the chart on page 22 or 141 will give you a more accurate reading.

SPECIFIC GRAVITY & POTENTIAL ALCOHOL

You can determine both the specific gravity and potential alcohol by using the saccharometer or you can determine the specific gravity and look up the potential alcohol on the chart on page 22.

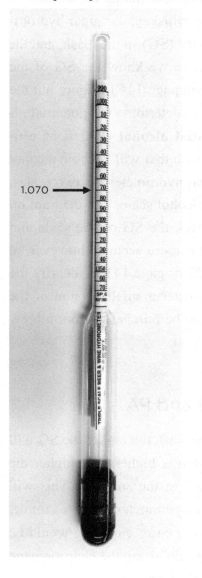

1.070 ➤

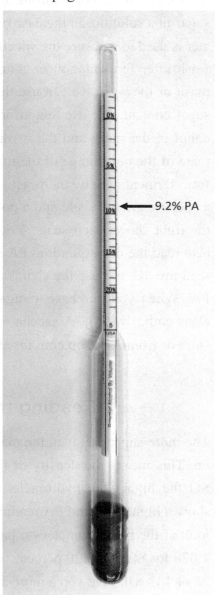

◀ 9.2% PA

Temperature (F°) Correction

The saccharometer is calibrated to work at a temperature of 20°C (68°F). You need to know the temperature of your wort or your wash when taking a measurement. Use your long stem food thermometer to take the temperature. If the wort or wash is higher or lower the 20°C (68°F) use the chart shown below to adjust your reading. Most saccharometers come with this chart.

54.2	**- 0.002**
61.5	**- 0.001**
68.0	**-**
73.7	**+ 0.001**
79.2	**+ 0.002**
84.3	**+ 0.003**

SPECIFIC GRAVITY & POTENTIAL ALCOHOL

Specific Gravity (20ºC/68ºF)	Potential Alcohol (%/Volume)
1.000	0.0
1.005	0.7
1.010	1.3
1.015	2.0
1.020	2.6
1.025	3.3
1.030	4.0
1.035	4.6
1.040	5.3
1.045	5.9
1.050	6.6
1.055	7.2
1.060	7.9
1.065	8.6
1.070	9.2
1.075	9.9
1.080	10.5
1.085	11.2
1.090	11.8
1.095	12.5
1.100	13.2
1.110	14.0

GRADUATED CYLINDER

The graduated cylinder is a necessary tool for using your hydrometers to measure specific gravity of your mash, wash and distillate. Remember that you are measuring the sugar content of your mash and wash in order to determine their potential alcohol. You are also measuring the abv of your distillate as you distill your wash. Fill the cylinder with fluid from your mash, your wash, or distillate from your still and place the appropriate hydrometer into the cylinder. A turkey baster works good for transferring fluid into the cylinder. Be sure to spin the hydrometer to eliminate any bubbles sticking to it. Just give it a slight spin, let it stop and take your reading. You can get a good graduated cylinder from Amazon.com for about $10.00.

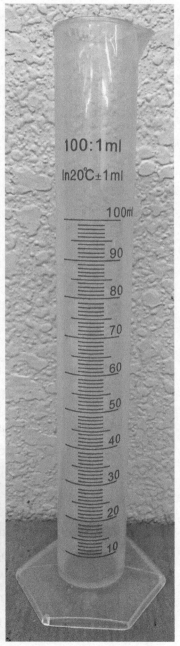

IODINE

Iodine can be used to conduct a quick test to determine the presence of starch in a mash or wort . This test can be used to determine if starch conversion in the mash is complete. Iodine reacts with the starch and produces a dark blue/black color. If no starch is present the color will be the orange/brown of the iodine. The iodine test will not show a reaction with simple carbohydrates or sugars.

Supplies Needed:
Iodine
Dropper
White plate

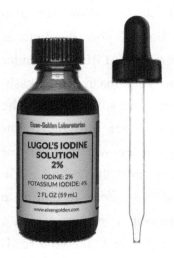

Procedure:
Take a few drops of wort and place it on a white plate.
Take a few drops of iodine and drop onto the wort.
Swirl it around a bit to mix.
Observe the color.

If you do an iodine test and find that there is still unconverted starch in your mash or wort, you will need to allow more time for saccharification. Heat your mash back to the correct temperature, stir it up some more, and let it rest for another hour or so. Test it again.

FIFTEEN GALLON COOKING POT WITH LID

The size of your cooking pot will depend on the size of your still and on how big of batches you plan to cook. I recommend a fifteen gallon, triple clad bottom pot. This will allow you to cook batches for a nine gallon (35 liter) still. Get a good quality pot with a triple clad bottom. The thick bottom of a pot like this will help prevent burning your mash on the bottom. A good quality cooking pot can be purchased at a brew store for about $85.00.

FOOD GRADE LONG STEM THERMOMETER

Used to check temperature of mash and distillate. Long stem thermometers are available at brew stores and online for $10.00.

LARGE STIRRING PADDLE/MASH PADDLE

A nice large stirring paddle makes mash cooking much easier. You can also use large stirring spoons, but if you do, stirring your mash will be a lot more work. You can find a metal or wooden paddle, like the one pictured, on-line for about $15.00.

PROPANE BURNER AND 5 GALLON TANK

The Bayou Country Classic propane burner is perfect for cooking large batches of mash. These are available at stores like Walmart, Lowe's, brew stores and online. They cost about $60.00. Propane tanks are available everywhere. They cost about $45.00.

EIGHT OUNCE CANNING JARS

You will need around twenty-four 8 ounce canning jars. These will be used during the spirit run. The **spirit run** is the second distillation you will do on each batch. It is the run where you will be collecting the final product and dividing it into four ounce increments as you distill. This process will be explained in full detail in the whiskey chapter. You can get canning jars at any department store for about $10.00 for a case of twelve.

ONE GALLON AGING JARS

Gallon jars are used to collect distillate during your stripping run and can be used to store and age your moonshine, if you decide to age any of it. Moonshine is not normally aged, but I think aging with uncharred oak improves the final product. In the chapter on aging we will discuss the jar aging method that is an alternative to aging in oak barrels. I recommend buying four or five of them to start with. You can get them at brew stores for $7.00

AGING JAR LABELS

It is really important to accurately label your aging jars or things will get mixed up and you won't know what you have in each jar. Make photocopies of the labels below and use them for labeling your jars. These could be used for any kind of spirit you make.

Batch No._____

Type of Spirit_____

Distillation Date_____

Mash Bill

_____

_____

Aging Proof_____

Batch No._____

Type of Spirit_____

Distillation Date_____

Mash Bill

_____

_____

Aging Proof_____

YEAST

When choosing a yeast for moonshine, you should consider the type of mash you'll be making. Some yeasts work better with simple sugars and fruits, while others are better for grain-based mashes. Some yeasts bring out the flavor of the raw materials, while others have a neutral flavor profile. We will look at a few yeast examples.

DISTILLER'S ACTIVE DRY YEAST (DADY)

There are many types of yeast in the Saccharomyces cerevisiae species that are used for distilling. DADY is a good all-purpose yeast that is good for making moonshine and other spirits. This yeast will consistently produce eight to ten percent alcohol depending on the mash bill. Yeasts produce various compounds, including esters, during fermentation, that give the distillate different flavors. Once you become a seasoned distill-

er you can experiment with different yeast strains. I think it's a good idea to start with DADY because it is reliable and far less expensive than other specialty yeast strains. You can buy it from brew stores or online for about $15.00 a pound. This is enough for many batches depending on the size of your still.

YEAST NUTRIENTS

DIAMMONIUM PHOSPHATE (DAP)

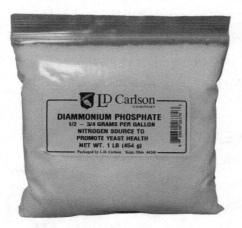

DAP is a good source of nitrogen and will help keep the yeast active during fermentation. It is recommended for juice washes and high sugar washes that do not contain grain. High sugar washes include things like plain sugar, molasses for rum, and agave syrup for tequila. DAP is added prior to fermentation at the same time yeast is pitched. Grain mash contains enough nitrogen to make the addition of DAP unnecessary. Be carful because too much nitrogen can harm and even kill yeast. The only reason I include DAP here is in case you decide to make some kind of fruit or sugar based moonshine, with no grain, which you can certainly do.

BALANCED YEAST NUTRIENTS

There are many so-called balanced yeast nutrients on the market. They contain a blend of minerals, proteins, amino acids, and vitamins that improves yeast activity during fermentation. They keep the yeast healthy and can prevent stuck fermentations. I have used many different brands over the years and my favorite is **Fermax**, made by BSG.

FERMAX YEAST NUTRIENT

Fermax Yeast Nutrient is a powder that contains diammonium phosphate, magnesium sulfate, yeast hulls, B vitamins, and calcium salts. It also contains a proprietary product called "Yeastade 50", which is autolyzed yeast that supplements the nutrient with vitamins, minerals, and amino acids. Note that it does contain some DAP. It will promote rapid starting of fermentation, help complete fermentation, improve attenuation, and create a healthy yeast population.

Rate: To begin a fermentation or restart a stuck fermentation, use 1 to 1.5 teaspoons per gallon of mash. Mix it in right before you pitch the yeast.

ENZYMES

Enzymes are important proteins that act as biological catalysts (biocatalysts). Catalysts accelerate chemical reactions but are not consumed in the reactions. The molecules which enzymes act on are called substrates. The enzymes convert the substrates into different molecules known as products. During the mashing process enzymes are needed to help convert starches into fermentable sugars, this is know as **saccharification**. The required enzymes are provided by using malted barley in most cases. Malted barley, and other malted grains, provide four primary enzymes. They include alpha-amylase, beta-amylase, maltase, and limit dextrinase. These enzymes are produced by the grain (seed) during germination or sprouting. The enzymes **hydrolyze** the starches in the endosperm of the grain converting them into glucose that can be use as a food source by the newly germinating embryo. In the malting process utilized by commercial malting companies grains are moistened to allow germination to begin and then they are heated to stop germination. This process of "malting" preserves the enzymes so that we can use them for saccharification during the mashing process. A significant amount of maltose, a sugar containing 2 glucose molecules, is produced during malting - thus the name **malted grain**. The term **diastase** is used to refer to any one of the enzymes involved in converting starches into simpler sugars. The amount of enzymes present in a malted grain is known as the **diastatic power (DP)**. It is a measurement of the combined power of the enzymes needed to hydrolyze starch. The unit of measurement for DP is degrees **Lintner (°L).** It refers to the combined starch degrading power (potential) for a pound of malted grain. One pound of a malted grain needs at least 30 °L in order to convert the starches it contains into simple sugars like glucose. Although the primary grain used in making moonshine is corn, some barley malt is usually added to the mash to provide the enzymes necessary for saccharification. I also recommend adding some alpha-amylase enzyme to the mash as well.

ALPHA-AMYLASE ENZYME

Alpha amylase enzyme is released from the aleurone layer that surrounds the endosperm of a grain (seed) like barley. The endosperm of the grain contains the starches which are a source of energy for the germinating embryo. The enzyme hydrolyzes and breaks chemical bonds in starch molecules, which are long chains of glucose molecules, into many smaller chains. The smaller chains are then exposed to further digestion by beta amylase enzyme. Many distillers add commercial alpha amylase enzyme to their mashes just to make sure there's an adequate amount. Depending on the brand, the rate is usually about ½ tsp per 5 gallons of mash. Check the instructions on the package.

Optimal Temperature: 66-71°C (150-160°F)
Optimal pH: 5.3-5.7

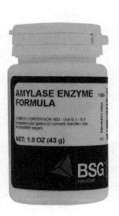

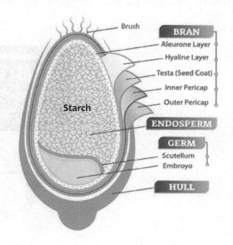

BETA-AMYLASE ENZYME

Beta amylase enzyme is produced in the endosperm of grains during germination. The enzyme can degrade and break apart amylose (a type of starch) and dextrins. It breaks the second chemical bond in a starch molecule and produces molecules of maltose. Maltose is composed of 2 glucose molecules.

Optimal Temperature: 54-66°C (129-150°F)
Optimal pH: 5.1-5.3

MALTASE ENZYME

Maltase is also found in malted grains. It will break the bonds of the maltose sugar, which is a **disaccharide**, and produce two molecules of glucose.

GLUCO-AMYLASE ENZYME

Glucoamylase is a **exogenous** enzyme that hydrolyzes short chain dextrins into fermentable sugars. This enzyme is not found in malted grains and is not needed unless you are preparing a mash of raw grains (not malted) or other starch based substrates like potatoes. Glucoamylase can be purchased at brew stores or online if needed.

FERMENTER

There are many types of fermenters available. There are fermenters with a basic snap-on lid, like the one shown below, and fermenters with an airtight lid and airlock. There are different opinions about which type to use. I prefer the snap-on lid style, they seem to work just fine for making moonshine.

12 GALLON FERMENTER WITH SNAP-ON LID

The snap-on lid will keep contaminants like wild yeast and bacteria out of your fermenter. It will also help keep extra oxygen out unless you open it frequently and/or slosh the contents around a lot. During active yeast fermentation a great deal of carbon dioxide is released which keeps oxygen from entering the fermenting mash. In addition, with grain mashes and anything with pulp, a fermentation cap forms on top of the mash and seals the fermenting contents below, so oxidation is minimal. I personally like the basic fermenter with a snap-on lid. I have used this type for fermenting moonshine mash, all-grain whiskey mashes, vodka, gin, rum, fruit brandy, and everything in between with no problems.

MASH BAG

The mash bag is placed inside your fermenting bucket. After you have cooked your mash, it has cooled to about 24°C (75°F), you have pitched the yeast, mixed it well, and aerated the mash, you pour the mash into the bag. This makes it easy to remove the mash from the fermenting bucket once fermentation is complete. This will be covered in detail in chapter 5.

AQUARIUM PUMP

There are different ways to aerate your mash. I have grown to like the aquarium pump method. First sterilize the tubing. Then, tie a weight to the end of the tube so it will sit on the bottom of your fermenter. Turn the pump on and let it aerate for 15 minutes. Works great.

FOOD SCALE

A good food scale is necessary for weighing your grain.

PLASTIC BOWL

A basic plastic salad or mixing bowl works well for measuring and weighing your grain, transferring grain into your cooking pot, transferring mash into your fermenter and for transferring your wash into your still.

KITCHEN STRAINER

A kitchen strainer is useful for taking samples of your wort when checking specific gravity. Place it into the mash pot to separate the wort from the grains.

FLOUR FOR SEALING THE STILL HEAD

You will need to make a **flour paste** for sealing your still head. The head is removeable and must be sealed when distilling to prevent vapor loss. Mix 1 Tbs of flour with about 1 Tbs of water and mix.

FERMENTATION ROOM

A small storage room is a great place for fermenting your batches of mash. Some distillers will use a closet, but fermentation can get messy so I advise against it. A small storage room works great. You have more room for you buckets and other supplies and you can easily heat the room with a small space heater. In the storage room shown below, a trailer winch is mounted to a beam and makes it easy to pull the mash bag, which can be quite heavy, from the fermenter when fermentation is complete.

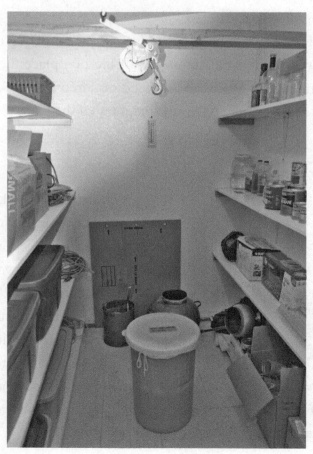

HOME-MADE MASH PRESS

When you pull your mash bag from the fermenter you have to allow it to drain. When it is finished draining, there will still be some wash remaining in the grain that will need to be squeezed out some-how. One method that works pretty well is to make a mash press. The  one pictured uses a livestock water tub, a plastic milk jug crate, and a block of wood. Put the crate on top of the tub, place the mash bag into the crate, place the block of wood on top of the mash bag, and stand on it. Your weight will press out more of the wort.

WORT CHILLER

 A wort chiller is optional, but it is a nice piece of equipment to have. After your mash has been cooked and rested for 90 minutes you need to cool it down to 24 to 27°C (75 to 80°F) before pitching your yeast. A good wort chiller can chill your wort down to yeast pitching temperature in 15 to 30 minutes depending on the volume of your mash. Another option is to place your cooking pot into a large barrel or sink full of cold water.

pH METER

Used to check the pH of your mash and your wort. A good quality pH meter is a good investment. Correct pH is important for mash saccharification and yeast fermentation. This is a really nice pH meter from Apera Instruments, Item No. AI209 PH20. They run about $50 at Amazon.

PRODUCT RECORD

Batch Number_____ **Name**_____

Grain Bill

_____

_____

_____

Mash

Date_____ Time_____Water Qty_____ Mash Vol._____

Heat water to 167°F. Add corn, mix, gelatinize, 158 - 167°F, 60 min.

Heat mash back to 158°F. Add other grains, amylase enzyme, mix.

Check pH (want 5.2 - 5.7) _____ Adjusted pH_____

Rest at 148F, 90 minutes, or over night_____

Cool to 75 - 80F

Check SG: OG _____, PA_____

Fermentation

Date_____Time_____

Check mash pH (want 4.0 - 4.5) _____ Adjusted pH _____

Starting OG _____, PA _____

Add yeast nutrients, mix _____, Qty _____

Add DAP (if needed), mix, Qty _____

Pitch yeast, mix _____, Qty _____

Aerate the mash

Pour into fermenter - Keep fermentation room between 70-80°F.

1st SG check: Date _____, SG _____

2nd SG check: Date _____, SG _____

Terminal Gravity: Date _____, TG _____

Fermentation end date _____, TG _____,PA _____

Net PA _____

Stripping Run
Heat slowly. Run to 96°C or 10% abv. Approx. 8 Hours. Low Wines.

Date_____ Start Time_____ End Time_____

1st Drips: Time_____ Distillate Temp_____

Fast Drips: Time_____ Distillate Temp_____

Starting abv_____ Time_____ Distillate Temp_____

Ending abv_____ Time_____ Distillate Temp_____

Final Blended abv _____ Qty_____

Spirit Run

Date _____ Start Time _____

Low wines abv _____ Water added _____ Adjusted abv _____

Foreshots amount collected _____ Dumped _____

Jar No.   Time   Temp   abv   Notes
_____
_____
_____

Jar No.	Time	Temp	abv	Notes

Heads cut: abv _____ Temp _____

Tails cut: abv _____ Temp _____

Total Volume _____ abv _____

Aging

Start date _____ End date _____

Quantity _____ abv _____ Aging Proof _____

Barrel _____

Toasted Wood Chips _____

Charred Wood Chips _____

Bottling

Date _____

Volume _____ Bottled Proof _____

Final Notes

_____

_____

_____

_____

_____

_____

_____

_____

_____

_____

_____

MISCELLANEOUS SUPPLIES

Space Heater with thermostat

A small space heater with a thermostat makes it easy to control the temperature in your fermentation chamber or room.

5 Gallon Buckets

You will need two 5 gallon buckets for aerating your mash and transferring your fermented wash into your still.

Storage Tub with Lid

A plastic tub works great for storing your supplies like hydrometers and other small items.

Plastic Garbage Can with Lid

A large garbage can is necessary to store your grains in.

Plastic Funnel

A plastic funnel is used to pour your whiskey into bottles.

Shop Rags

Shop rags will be used throughout the whiskey making process.

Rope

You will need about 6 feet of 3/8" rope to tie to your mash bag when it is ready to pull from the fermenter.

Measuring Spoons - Tbs, tsps, etc.

Sharpie

Use a sharpie to record your temperature and abv when distilling and for labeling your fermenters when fermenting.

Coffee Filters

Coffee filters are used to filter your moonshine if you plan to age it.

16 Ounce Measuring Cup

You will need a measuring cup to measure the quantity of your distillate.

Cleaning Station, Hose

A wood bench, hose and running water are nice to have for cleaning and rinsing your equipment.

Bleach

Bleach is used to sanitize your non-copper tools and equip.

White Vinegar

Vinegar works well for cleaning your still, alcohol parrot and anything made of copper.

Star Sans

Used to disinfect tools and equipment.

PBW (Powdered Brewery Wash)

Used for cleaning still, tools, equipment.

Scrubber Pads or Scrubber Brush

Scrubber pads or a scrubber brush will work well for cleaning your still and other equipment.

Sixteen Gallon Tub

Used to make a home-made mash press. Available at livestock feed stores. About $15.00.

Milk Crate

For home-made mash press.

Thick Piece of Wood

For home-made mash press.

3

Cleaning and Sanitizing Equipment

S anitation is obviously important when cooking and fermenting. This chapter includes some sanitation products to use and some tips on keeping your equipment clean.

CLEANING NON-COPPER EQUIPMENT

Bleach

Use about 1 tbsp of bleach per gallon of water for cleaning/sanitizing your non-copper equipment. Do not use bleach on cooper items, it will corrode the metal. Use a bleach solution for your stainless steel still, mash cooking pot, five gallon buckets, fermenter and lid, mixing paddle, jars and plastic bowl. Just wipe down the items with the bleach solution and triple rinse. Rinsing three times is a good practice to make sure all of the bleach solution is removed from the item being cleaned. You should sanitize all equipment before each new batch.

CLEANING COPPER EQUIPMENT

White Vinegar

Use white vinegar and water to clean your still, condenser and alcohol parrot. It is a good cleaner, but does not sanitize. In realty, your copper still gets sanitized every time you heat it while distilling.

Outside of Still

Mix 1 tbsp of salt, 1 cup white vinegar and enough flour to make a paste.
Apply to the outside of your still.
Let it sit for 30 minutes.
Wash off with cloth and water.

Inside of Still - Light Cleaning

A light cleaning is all that is necessary most of the time.
Put about 1 gallon of water and 2 cups of vinegar into your still.
Scrub out the still with a scrubber pad or brush.
Triple rinse. Do a light cleaning before each new batch.

Outside of Still

Mix 1 tbsp of salt, 1 cup white vinegar and enough flour to make a paste.
Apply to the outside of your still.
Let it sit for 30 minutes.
Wash off with cloth and water.

Inside of Still - Light Cleaning

A light cleaning is all that is necessary most of the time.
Put about 1 gallon of water and 2 cups of vinegar into your still.
Scrub out the still with a scrubber pad or brush.
Triple rinse. Do a light cleaning before each new batch.

Inside of Still- Thorough Cleaning

After every 10 distillation runs I recommend a thorough cleaning. Put 2 gallons of water and 2 gallons of vinegar into your still. Put the still head on, connect your condenser and run the still. Heat the solution up to boiling and let it run through your system for 10 minutes. Don't forget to set up a collection jar or you'll have hot vinegar water all over the floor. Triple rinse.

STAR SAN

Star San is an acid-based no-rinse sanitizer that is effective and easy to use. It is made from food-grade phosphoric acid, safe for people and the environment. Star San is self-foaming which helps it to penetrate cracks and crevices. It is odorless and flavorless, and does not require rinsing when used at the recommended dilution. Use only 1 oz Star San per 5 gallons of water and just 1 to 2 minutes of contact time. Used as a soaking solution, it can also be applied by hand (wear gloves) or with a spray bottle. It is also reusable. A solution of Star San will remain effective for up to three to four weeks in a sealed container; it is effective as long as the pH is 3 or lower.

PBW

PBW (Powdered Brewery Wash) is a patented alkali cleaner originally developed for Coors, now widely used in commercial breweries across North America. Use 1 to 2 ounces per gallon for cleaning kettles, 3/4 ounce per gallon for fermenters, kegs, tanks, and other equipment. Soak equipment overnight in PBW solution; rinse the following morning - no scrubbing required!

4

Setting Up Your Distillery

It is important to have a distillery that is efficient and safe. I would avoid distilling inside your house. Some distillers use their kitchen as a distilling area. In my opinion, this practice is not affective and can be dangerous. It is best to have a separate distilling area in a shed or shop building. In this chapter we will look at some suggestions for a good distillery setup.

Requirements of a Good Distillery

Distillery Location
I recommend using a separate building for your distillery. A shed or shop is a good place for a home distillery.

Lockable
Be sure the space you use for your distillery can be locked.

Airflow
Good air flow is required when cooking and distilling, especially if you are using propane as your heat source. Windows and/or doors should be located near your distillery.

Water Source
Water is obviously important in distilling. If you have water inside the building you are using that's a bonus. If not, you can pull in a garden hose from outside. Another option is to plumb in a water line using black PVC irrigation tubing. You can get PVC tubing, connectors, and valves at any home improvement store.

Lighting
Good lighting is another essential feature of a good distillery. You will be reading hydrometers, checking pH levels, measuring enzymes, yeast nutrients, and yeast, and recording data in your distilling records - all of this requires adequate lighting.

Cooking Area

Your cooking area should have enough space for grain storage, a large cooking pot, burner, enzymes, yeast nutrients, measuring scale, batch record book, and the various tools required for cooking mash as covered in chapter 2.

Distilling Area

You will also need space for your still, condenser, and distillate collection jars. A water line is shown coming in from the left and connected to the condenser.

Fermentation Room

A room dedicated to fermentation is a nice feature of a distillery. In this room you will ferment your batches of whiskey mash and extract the fermented wash when fermentation is complete. Controlling ambient temperature is also much easier in a dedicated room. If you don't have a room to use you could build a fermentation chamber out of plywood.

Aging and Storage

An old bookshelf works well for storing and/or aging gallons of moonshine, whiskey, or whatever else you are making.

A Picture of the Entire Distillery

The table on the left is used to hold the condenser and gallon jars used during the stripping run. Moving to the right, you have the short little table that holds the pot still. It is the correct height to place the still at the same level as the condenser. To the right of the pot still is another table that holds various supplies. This table is used during the spirit run to hold mason jars full of distillate. There is also a stainless steel column still stored on this table. The counter at the right is a place for cooking supplies and a product record notebook. At the far right is the cooking pot, burner, propane tank, and plastic garbage can for grain storage.

5

How to Make Moonshine

In the past making moonshine was a risky pursuit. With crude stills and equipment, and a lack of proper safety guidelines, people could easily be poisoned. Some went blind and others died from consuming toxic substances like methanol. Today things are quite different. By utilizing modern distilling equipment and following proper production practices, making moonshine is safe and rewarding. Also be reminded that making moonshine without a license is illegal.

In this chapter we will cover the entire moonshine production process. This will include grain selection, enzymes, pH levels, yeast nutrients, yeast, cooking mash, fermentation, distilling, aging (if desired), and bottling. We will examine an example batch of moonshine from start to finish. This will give you a good understanding of the entire process and prepare you for making your own high quality shine.

MOONSHINE GRAIN BILL AND RECIPE

Moonshine can technically be made of any kind of fermentable carbohydrate source; grain, fruit, or vegetable. The traditional moonshine grain bill is composed of corn, barley malt, water, yeast, and sometimes sugar. The corn provides the primary source of starch (carbohydrates), the barley malt provides a source of enzymes needed for starch conversion to sugar (saccharification), sugar can be used to increase the potential alcohol content, and the yeast ferments the mash. Adding sugar will dilute the overall flavor profile of the moonshine and can be harmful to yeast health if too much is added. Careful consideration must be given to the actual ingredients used and the quantity of each. Following the grain bills and guidelines in this chapter will ensure that you have a successful moonshine production process. We will be using the 8 gallon pot still for our examples. If you have a still of a different volume you can easily adjust the recipe.

Basic Moonshine Recipe

Water - 8 Gallons
Corn Meal - 80%, 19.2 pounds
Barley Malt - 20%, 4.8 pounds
Alpha-amylase Enzyme - 1 tsp
Glucoamylase Enzyme - 1 tsp (not required, but may increase starch conversion)
Fermax Yeast Nutrient - 10 tsp
Distiller's Active Dry Yeast (DADY) - 5 tsp

---

* *If you use a different yeast nutrient or a different yeast strain,
  follow the rate on the package.*

PREPARING THE MASH

1. Put 8 Gallons of Water in the Cooking Pot

2. Heat the Water to 75ºC (167ºF)

3. Add the Corn and Gelatinize

For any mash bill that includes corn meal or cracked corn, the corn must be gelatinized. Flaked corn does not need to be gelatinized. Put in 19.2 lb. of corn meal. Stir constantly as you add the corn or you will get corn dough balls that are hard to mix in. Once it is well mixed, put the lid on the pot and let it sit for one hour. You want to keep the temperature between 70ºC (158ºF) and 75ºC (167ºF). The corn mash will get very thick. It will liquefy after you mix in the barley malt and amylase enzyme later on. Add heat to the mash if necessary in order to keep the temperature up.

4. Add the Barley Malt

Heat the mash back to 70ºC (158ºF).

Add 4.8 lb. of barley malt, stir it into the mash.

Once you mix in the barley malt the temperature will drop to approximately 148ºF, this is where you want to be. Add some heat if necessary.

5. Add the Alpha-amylase Enzyme

Alpha-amylase enzyme is added at the rate of ½ teaspoon per 5 gallons of mash. For this batch of 10 gallons add 1 teaspoon. Mix everything together well. A few minutes of good mixing will do.

6. Check the pH of Your Mash

Place your kitchen strainer into the top of the mash. Draw a sample of work with the turkey baster. Place the wort into a graduated cylinder and wait for the temperature of the sample to drop to about 24°C (75° F). Next, place your pH meter into the sample and take a reading. pH stands for potential hydrogen. pH measures the acidity and alkalinity of a substance. We are concerned about the pH of our mash, and our wort prior to fermentation. The pH scale is a logarithmic scale that goes from 0 to 14. Seven is neutral, anything below 7 is acidic, and anything above 7 is alkaline. Acidic substances have a high concentration of hydrogen ions (H^+) and alkaline substances have a high concentration of hydroxyl ions (OH^-). **In the distilling business the optimum pH for mash is between 5.2 and 5.7, moderately acidic.** This pH range improves the activity of the enzymes responsible for saccharification and gives us a better conversion of the starches in the mash to glucose. The good news is that mash can naturally be in the pH range of 5.2 to 5.7 because grains are acidic by nature. But, this is not always the case depending on the particular mash bill you are cooking. The water you are using or the particular grains you are using can often produce a pH value that is above the optimum range. **You can easily lower the pH by adding citric acid, lactic acid, gypsum, phosphoric acid, lemon juice, or 5.2 pH Stabilizer to your mash.** Add 1 teaspoon at a time, mix it in, then recheck your pH. **If you have a pH that is too low, you can add lime (calcium carbonate, $CaCO_3$) or baking soda (sodium bicarbonate, $NaCO_3$) to your mash; this will raise the pH.**

Using a kitchen strainer and turkey baster to draw a wort sample.

Taking a wort pH reading with a pH meter. Be sure to let the wort sample temperature drop to room temperature before taking the reading. pH should be between 5.2 and 5.7 for efficient saccharification.

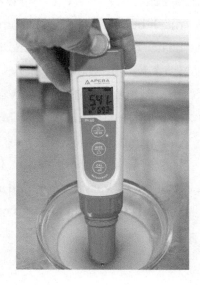

7. Rest the Mash for 90 Minutes

Place the lid on your pot and let the mash rest for 90 minutes. You only need to keep the temperature at 64°C (148°F) for 90 minutes. This is where saccharification is occurring and the starches are being converted into glucose - also known as conversion. The glucose is the simple sugar which will be fermented by the yeast during fermentation.

8. Cool the Mash

Next, we need to cool the mash down to **24°C to 27°C (75°F to 80°F).** You can use a wort chiller after 90 minutes or you can let the mash rest overnight. The goal is to allow the temperature to drop down to the correct temperature range before pitching the yeast. If you're going to leave it overnight just bring it to 64°C (148°F) then let it rest until the next morning. When the temperature drops to about 24°C to 27°C (75°F to 80°F) you can pitch your yeast.

9. Check the Specific Gravity of the Wort

Do this before pitching the yeast. Once the wort has cooled to between 24 and 27°C (75 and 80°F), place your kitchen strainer into the mash bucket to separate some wort from the grain. Using your turkey baster draw some wort and place it into your graduated cylinder. Fill it to within about 3 inches of the top. Use your saccharometer to check the specific gravity of the wort. It should read somewhere around 1.080, this is your **original gravity (OG),** which equates to a **potential alcohol (PA)** of 10.5%. Your actual OG could be a little less or a little more. Your PA should be between 8 and 12%. Every batch will vary by a small amount. Not to worry. Record your OG and PA in your distillation record.

The saccharometer is placed into the wort which is in the graduated cylinder. The reading appears to show a specific gravity of about 1.080. If we check the chart of page 141 we can see that a 1.080 SG would be a potential alcohol of 10.5%. Between 8 and 12% PA is good.

FERMENTATION

Fermentation is the process of converting sugars, like glucose and maltose, into acids, carbon dioxide (CO_2) and various alcohols by yeasts. Putting yeast into the mash or the wort, so they can consume glucose and produce alcohol, is called pitching the yeast. The alcohol we are primarily interested in is ethanol (C_2H_5OH). During both respiration and fermentation yeast cells break down glucose molecules to release energy. This is called glycolysis. The breakdown of glucose also releases carbon atoms which can be used by the yeast to grow and reproduce (budding). There are two primary methods of fermentation used in distilling alcohol, **fermenting on the grain** and **fermenting off the grain**. When fermenting on the grain, the yeast is pitched into the mash which is transferred to a fermenter. When fermenting off the grain, the wort is first separated from the mash and the yeast is pitched into the wort for fermentation. Moonshine mash bills that contain corn are usually fermented on the grain.

1. Sanitize Your Fermentation Equipment

See page 49 for complete information on sanitizing and cleaning equipment.

2. Place a Mash Big in Your Fermenter and Tie

It's a good idea to have the mash bag in place and ready to go.

3. Check the pH of the Mash

Before you pitch your yeast and start fermentation you should check your mash pH again. Yeast do best when the pH of your mash is moderately acidic. **The best pH range is from 4.0 to 4.5.** This pH range keeps the yeast healthy and helps control undesirable bacterial growth. You can easily lower the pH by adding citric acid, lactic acid, gypsum, phosphoric acid, lemon juice, or 5.2 pH Stabilizer to your mash. Add 1 teaspoon at a time, mix it in, then recheck your pH. If you have a pH that is too low, you can add lime (calcium carbonate) or baking soda (sodium bicarbonate) to your mash. This will raise the pH.

4. Add Yeast Nutrients

The source of energy consumed by yeast is glucose, but yeast also requires other nutrients in order to reproduce and grow. Yeast nutrient blends contain a mix of trace elements, inorganic nitrogen, organic nitrogen, zinc, phosphates, and B vitamins that help yeast grow and complete fermentation. Yeast nutrients are added to the mash at the same time as the yeast is pitched. You need 1 teaspoon of Fermax yeast nutrients per gallon of mash. Put **10 teaspoons** into your mash and mix it in well. If you are using a different nutrient, follow the instructions on the package.

5. Pitch the Yeast

The next step is to add yeast, otherwise known as pitching the yeast. **Use 1/2 tsp of Distiller's Active Dry Yeast or DADY per gallon of mash.** Get your yeast from the refrigerator, place 5 teaspoons in a small plastic bag or bowl and let it warm to room temperature for about 15 minutes. Then add it to your cooled mash and mix it in. Be sure the mash has been cooled to **24°C to 27°C (75°F to 80°F).**

Yeast Starter

Another method is to create a yeast starter. This will get the yeast off to a quick start and also let you know if you have healthy active yeast prior to pitching. Add 1 teaspoon of sugar to 1 cup of warm water (43°C, 110°F), add your yeast, mix it up and let it sit for about 15 minutes. The yeast should form a nice head of foam (barm) on top. This indicates healthy, active yeast. Then, pitch the yeast starter into your wort.

6. Aerate the Mash

After mixing, the mash should be aerated by pouring it back and forth between two five gallon buckets three times. This introduces more oxygen into the mash for the yeast to utilize. You can also use an aquarium pump with a tube to aerate the mash. Remove the mash using your plastic bowl. It is much easier to do it with a bowl in small amounts rather than trying to lift and pour your whole cooking pot. Pour bowls of mash into a 5 gallon bucket until the bucket is about half full. Next pour the mash between your two five gallon buckets three times. This will aerate the mash. After aerating pour the half bucket into your fermenter. Keep doing this until the mash pot is empty and all of the mash is in your fermenter.

7. Pour the Mash into the Fermenter

After aerating, pour the mash into the fermenter.

8. Put the Lid on the Fermenter and Label it

On the label I like to include the date, batch number, product name, and OG.

9. Put the Fermenter in Your Fermentation Room

Set your heater at 24 to 27°C (75 to 80°F) and close the door.

PROCEDURES DURING FERMENTATION

1. Check for the Grain Cap and Crackling Sound

Check your batch after the first 2 to 3 hours. Pull the lid off of the fermenter. You should see the grain cap. When the yeast really start growing and producing CO_2, a grain cap will form at the top of the fermenter. This is a good sign because it shows that the yeast are actively fermenting. You should also be able to hear a distinct crackling sound, like Rice Krispies in a bowl of milk.

Grain Cap

2. Monitor the Temperature of Your Fermentation Room

Check the temperature of your fermentation chamber each day. You want it to stay around 24° to 27°C (75° to 80°F).

3. Check the Specific Gravity of the Wash

Check the SG every couple of days with your saccharometer. When the SG drops to 1.000, or close to it, fermentation is complete. Fermentation should be complete in about 3 or 4 days. At his point all or most of the glucose has been converted to alcohol and the yeast are beginning to flocculate (clump together) and go dormant. You will not the hear the crackling sound any longer and the grain cap may have sunk back into the wash. Dormant yeast, lees, will settle out and will be building up on the bottom of your fermenter. Fermentation is complete at this point. It's time to pull the mash bag and recover the wash.

What to do if Your Get a Stuck Fermentation

If, after a few days, your SG does not seem to be dropping, as it should when the sugars are being fermented by the yeast, you may have a stuck fermentation. This can happen for a variety of reasons, the most frequent of which is a lack of yeast nutrients. Simply add another does of nutrients and mix them in. Fermentation should start up once again.

RECOVERING THE WASH

The wort, which was the liquid with the mash, has been fermented and is now called the wash. It will normally contain between 8 and 10% alcohol. Our task now is to separate the wash from the mash and prepare for distillation. The picture shows the use of a trailer winch for pulling the mash bag from the fermenter - a really good method.

1. **Open the Fermenter and Tie a Rope Around the Top of the Mash Bag**

2. **Pull the Mash Bag Out of the Fermenter**

You can let it drain overnight or you can squeeze the liquid out of the mash bag. When it is finished draining you will end up with about 6.5 gallons of wash in your fermenter. After it settles you will see about an inch layer of material settled in the bottom, this is called trub. It consists of fats, proteins, dormant and dead yeast. The yeast that has also settled with the trub is called the lees.

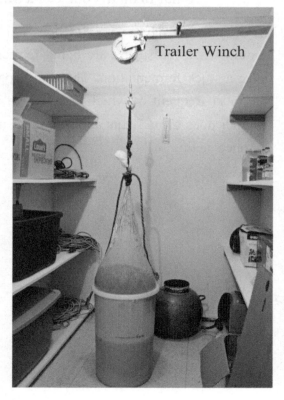

Trailer Winch

3. Press Out the Remaining Wash

There are many ways to squeeze out the last bit of wash, you can't get it all with your hands. You could use a home-made mash press like the one shown below or you can create your own method.

Livestock tub. Available at feed stores.

4. Allow the Wash to settle for Two Days

This will allow the wash to clear and allow dormant yeast to flocculate and settle on the bottom. Now you are ready for the stripping run.

5. Remove the Wash from the Fermenter

Begin ladling out the wash into a five gallon bucket with your plastic bowl or use a siphon. Fill the bucket about half way with wash. Pour the wash from the bucket into your still. Keep doing this until all of the wash is in the still. The normal practice is to leave the trub and lees in the bottom of the fermenter. Most distillers believe this material should not be placed into the still as it may cause off flavors in the distillate.

Using a bowl to remove the wash.

Using a siphon to remove the wash.

FIRST DISTILLATION
STRIPPING RUN

Distillation is the process of separating substances from a liquid mixture by heating, evaporating (forming a vapor), cooling and condensing vapor back into a liquid. Once the vapor is condensed back into a liquid it is referred to as the distillate. In the case of making whiskey the distillate is alcohol, primarily ethanol. The distillate produced during the moonshine making process starts off clear as water; this is true for any kind of spirit. The stripping run has the sole purpose of getting all of the alcohol out of the wash. That includes the good stuff and the not so good stuff. Follow the steps outlined in this section and your stripping run will be a success.

1. Pour the Wash into the Still
Each time you collect about half a bucket of wash pour it into your still. If your still is located close enough to your still you could just ladle or siphon the wash directly from the fermenter. Otherwise, moving the wash to the still with a 5 gallon bucket works very well.

2. Attach the Head onto the Still and Connect the Lyne Arm to the Condenser Tube

Place the still head on top of the still. Fasten the lyne arm to the condenser tube. If your still has a fastening nut for connecting the head tube to the condenser tube, tighten it by hand, doesn't need to be too tight. Using the side of your hand, lightly pound the still head into place on the still. You want the still head to sit squarely onto the still with the seam even all the way around.

3. Seal Still Head

Mix up some flour paste and seal your still head.

Flour Paste
1 Tablespoons flour
1 Tablespoon water

Sealing the Still Head

4. Set Up a One Gallon Collection Jar and the Alcohol Parrot

For the stripping run you will use a 1 gallon jar to collect the distillate. Place the jar on a small table or small wooden box so it sits below you condenser. Place the food grade condenser collection tube into the top of your parrot. Position the parrot tube so that distillate will flow into your gallon jar from the parrot. Place your alcoholometer inside the parrot as shown.

Alcoholometer

Food grade condenser tube bringing distillate from the still.

5. Turn on the Burner

The goal is to heat up the wash slowly. If you heat it up too fast you could burn the wash and you could vaporize the liquid too fast. This would result in too high a concentration of water coming through with your alcohol. So go slow! As the run progresses you will need to increase the temperature a little at a time. You will know it is time to increase the temperature when the distillate dripping rate slows way down. It will take 1½ to 2 hours before you see any distillate dripping from your collection tube, depending on the volume of your batch. Then things will speed up.

6. Turn on the Condenser Water Line

After turning on your burner turn on the water line to the condenser. Just a trickle will do. The water will slowly come in through the bottom waterline and will slowly trickle out of the top outlet line. This will keep your condenser water cool enough to liquefy the vapor coming from the still. You must make sure the incoming water is cold. Also make sure your outflow line is set up to drain outside or into some kind of drain.

7. Collect the Distillate (Low Wines)

You should see your first drips of distillate after about 1½ to 2 hours. The vapor temperature will be around 60°C (140°F). When your parrot fills with distillate you will be able to start observing the abv. It will start at around 75%. As the temperature rises up into the 70°C (158°F) range the distillate will start to drip faster. You want fast steady dripping, not a solid stream. Once your temperature reaches around 70°C (158°F) it will quite suddenly jump up towards the 80°C (176°F) area. As the drip rate slows slowly increase the heat to your still. The temperature will slowly increase and the abv will slowly decrease as the run continues. Monitor your abv and keep distilling until the abv has dropped to around 10%. Your vapor temperature will be around 95°C (203°F) at this point. You can distill all the way down to 0% abv, but there is not much alcohol at that point, mostly water. I recommend stopping the run at around 10% abv. The final combined abv of your distillate will be around 50%. Stripping runs normally produce distillate between 40 and 60% abv. This is called the low wines. You should get about 15 to 20% of your wash returned as low wines. Of course this will depend on when you decide to stop the run. If your final combined abv is above 40% you should add some filtered water to dilute the distillate down to below 40% abv before doing the spirit run (second distillation). You do not want to place a high abv charge into your still; 40% abv is flammable. This can be dangerous if you have a spill. The entire run for a 6.5 gallon wash will take about 7 hours.

Label your collection jars with the following: Stripping Run, Batch Number, Date. Keep these in a safe place until you are ready to do the spirit run.

Be sure to study the actual stripping run data for this batch on the next page. It will help clarify the stripping run process for you.

STRIPPING RUN DATA

Moonshine Batch

Distilled down to 20% abv

Total Volume of Low Wines Collected: 160 ounces

ABV: 53%

PROOF: 106

SECOND DISTILLATION
SPIRIT RUN NO. 1

This is an overview of the spirit run. We will cover the specific steps afterwards. First, clean out your still and place the distillate from the stripping run into your still. If your low wines are 40% abv or above, add a half gallon of water or so to your still. This will drop the low wines abv down into the thirties and make your distillation safer. The purpose of this run is to separate the different alcohols out and to isolate the ethanol, the good stuff, as much as possible. It is best to collect 4 ounces of distillate at a time in 8 ounce mason jars. You will need about 24 eight ounce jars, and maybe more, depending on the size of your batch. When the run is finished you will be able to make your cuts and separate the heads, hearts, and tails by analyzing each jar. This will be explained step-by-step on page 89. You want to heat your still slowly. You should control your burner temperature to ensure a steady drip of distillate, not a stream. If you start getting a stream, back off the heat a little bit. Three drips per second is good. Distilling too fast will make it harder to separate the different alcohols from the run. You should see your first slow drips of distillate after about 30 minutes. The vapor temperature will be around 60°C (140°F). The first few ounces of distillate are called the foreshots. These contain methanol, which is poisonous, and other undesirable alcohols that must be discarded. There is a lot of conflicting information about the quantity of foreshots to discard. Some distillers believe foreshots should be removed from both the stripping run and the spirit run. Others believe they should be removed from one or the other. I recommend discarding one ounce per gallon of original wash from the spirit run. You might be discarding a little more than you really need to, but you're just removing some early heads so it doesn't really matter, you probably don't want to keep them anyway; better to be on the safe side. So, if we had 7 gallons of wash after fermentation, we would discard the first 7 ounces of foreshots from the spirit run. Around 5% of your distillate will be foreshots. As the run continues the temperature will rise and the abv will decline, just like in the stripping run. However, the abv will be much higher to begin with, since you are now distilling a more concentrated solution. Within another 10 minutes or so your temperature will move up to about 70°C (158°F) and you will start seeing faster drips of distillate. At this point the distillate will be the heads of your run. The heads will normally have an abv of 80% and above. Heads can be discarded or kept and added to your next batch of low wines for distillation. The heads contain compounds like acetone, acetaldehyde, acetate and some ethanol. They have a strong, almost fruity smell and taste harsh. Approximately 20-30% of the liquid collected during a spirit distillation run will be heads. This will vary depending on the spirit being produced.

As you continue the run the temperature will suddenly rise to about 78°C (172°F) and you will have fast dripping distillate. This is where the hearts will begin. The hearts contain mainly ethanol and are the part of the spirit run we want to collect and make into whiskey. Hearts will have a light sweet smell and a light sweet, smooth taste. Be warned though, hearts still do not taste like whiskey, they are still raw distillate. The vapor temperature where the majority of the hearts will be boiling and vaporizing, will be between 78°C (172°F) and 82°C (179.6°F). But remember, there is still a considerable amount of ethanol coming out in your distillate at temperatures above that range, even as high as 90°C (194°F). The abv of your hearts will be below 80% and down to about 55% to 60% abv. This can vary depending on your equipment, the kind of spirit you are distilling, and many other variables. Monitoring your temperature and abv is important, but they are only a guideline for making your final cuts. The skill of the distiller is in developing the ability to smell and taste the different fractions of distillate in order to separate the heads, hearts and tails effectively. The first 4 ounces collected, in one of your 8 ounce mason jars, should have a vapor temperature of about 80°C (176°F) and an abv of about 80% (160 proof). As you continue to distill and collect distillate in 4 ounce amounts, the vapor temperature will slowly rise and the abv will slowly decline. Eventually you will have about 24 jars each filled with 4 ounces of distillate all lined up in a row on your table. Each will be labeled with their respective temperatures and abv's. Approximately 30-40% of the run will be hearts. The temperature will continue to rise and the abv to decline. As your temperature moves past 82°C (179.6°F) the quantity of ethanol in the distillate with begin to decline. As the temperature approaches 90°C (194°F) tails of the run will start to show up. The tails occur toward the end of the run. Tails do contain some ethanol as well as fusel oils like propanol, butanol and amyl alcohol. Tails also contain water, carbohydrates and proteins. You will know when the tails start because they smell like a wet dog and taste muddy. You may also see an oily sheen on surface of your distillate and it will start to look cloudy. Stop the run at about 96°C (205°F) or 20% abv. Tails will make up 20-30% of your run. Tails can be discarded or collected and added to the next spirit run. To make the cuts for the heads, hearts, and tails you need to consider the temperature, abv, aroma, and taste of each jar. The spirit run will take 3 to 4 hours to complete. In step 13 of the spirit run we will explain making the cuts in more detail.

STEPS FOR THE SPIRIT RUN

1. Clean Your Still

After the stripping run is finished you need to clean your still. You can use alcohol or white vinegar, but don't use bleach on anything made of copper. It will corrode the copper. I recommend vinegar. Pour about a pint of vinegar into your still, add a couple of gallons of water and scrub out your still with a dish scrubber pad. Rinse out your still 3 times with a hose. Do the same for your still head. You should also pour some vinegar through you alcohol parrot and rinse it out good.

The main thing you are getting rid of when cleaning your still is copper sulfate ($CuSO_4$). When you are distilling the vapors in the still contain sulfur. The sulfur binds with the copper your still is made of and creates copper sulfate. The copper sulfate binds to the interior of your still. This is a very beneficial reaction because it removes the sulfur from your distillate. This greatly improves the taste of your product. The only negative thing is you need to clean the copper sulfate out of your still after each use. Some vinegar, water and moderate scrubbing will do the job.

2. Put a Line of Duct Tape on Your Table

This will be for recording the temperature and abv for each of your small collection jars as the run progresses. It is important to collect the distillate in 4 ounce increments and record the temperature and abv. This will help you make the heads, hearts and tails cuts when the run is finished.

Duct tape placed on the edge of the table, ready for recording temperature and abv during the spirit run.

3. Get Your 8 Ounce Mason Jars Ready

Rinse out your jars and have them ready to go. Once the distillation gets going you will be filling jars and setting up new ones about every 10 minutes.

4. Pour the Low Wines into the Still

Take your low wines jars and pour them into your still. Your low wines should have an abv that is lower than 40%. Alcohol becomes flammable at 40% abv. If you have a batch of low wines that are 40% abv or higher, you should add some filtered water and dilute it down to below 40%. I like to add enough water to reduce the abv to 35%. *Use the dilution calculator at hillbillystills.com/distilling-calculators/265.htm*

For our example moonshine batch I added 82 ounces of water to the 160 ounces of low wines. This produced a low wines abv of 35%. This was the "charge" I placed in the still for the spirit run.

5. Put Your Still Back Together

Put the still head back on. Connect the lyne arm to the condenser. Re-seal the head with flour paste.

6. Set Up the Foreshots Collection Jar

This jar will be used to collect the first 7 ounces of our spirit run (for our 7 gallon wash example). *This will include the foreshots and should be dumped.* It will contain methanol and other undesirable alcohols. Remember to collect 1 ounce per gallon of original wash as foreshots. *Do not use your parrot to collect this first jar.* You don't want methanol in your parrot.

7. Turn on the Condenser Water Line

You want just a trickle of water coming in through your water line. The amount coming in must equal the amount going out through the outflow line on top of the condenser. The goal is to keep the water in the condenser cool.

8. Turn on the Burner

For the spirit run you can start off with medium heat and turn it down when the temperature begins to rise to about 70°C (158°F). Let the temperature rise slowly by adjusting your burner. You want each kind of alcohol to boil out slowly. Maintain a drip rate of 3 or 4 drips per second.

9. Collect the Foreshots

Remember, you are not using the alcohol parrot at this step. Collect the foreshots directly into your foreshots jar, the one you are going to dump. At about 60°C (140°F) you will start to see slow drips of distillate. It will take about half an hour for this to start. The temperature will slowly rise. Then the temperature will spike to around 78°C (172°F) and the speed of the drips of distillate will increase. You want fast dripping distillate, but not a steady stream. If you get a stream you will not be separating the different fractions of alcohol correctly. Turn the temperature down a little if this happens. When the first jar has close to 7 ounces of distillate in it get ready to pull it. I like to be on the safe side and recommend dumping 1 full ounce per gallon of wash which would be 7 ounces for our example batch. Dump this first jar and check it off on your product record sheet so you know you have completed this important step.

10. Put the Alcohol Parrot and First Jar in Place. Collect Distillate

After discarding the foreshots put your parrot under the distillate tube from your condenser. Put your first jar under the parrot tube to collect the distillate. It will take a few minutes for the parrot to fill with distillate and start dripping. This is helpful because it gives you some time to get your next jar in place. Put your alcoholom-

eter into the parrot. As the first jar fills your still vapor temperature will be around 80°C (176°F) and your abv will be around 80%. Monitor your burner and try to keep it around 80°C (176°F). As the run continues the temperature will slowly rise and the abv will slowly drop. Monitor your burner and adjust as necessary to keep a steady drip of distillate.

11. Collect Distillate in 4 Ounce Quantities and Record Data

As each jar fills to about half full, 4 ounces, replace the jar with an empty one and place the full one on your table by the duct tape. Check the temperature and abv for each jar and write them on the duct tape as shown below. As the spirit run progresses your table will look like the one in the picture. Mason jars about half full of distillate with their respective temperature and abv recorded on the duct tape.

12. Stopping the Spirit Run

There are several options for when to stop your spirit distillation run. You could continue to distill until there is zero alcohol coming out of your still, in other words, 0% abv. However, this is really not worth the effort as the distillate, at this point, is mostly water. If you decide to distill out most of the tails in the batch and put them into your next spirit run, you could distill down to 10% abv. If you don't want to keep the tails for the next distillation, you could stop the run at the point where you think the tails have started in the run, possibly as early 65% abv if you use the 75/65 cuts. I recommend distilling until 10% abv and keeping the tails to put into the next spirit run. The reason for doing this is that there is still some ethanol in the tails that could be recovered in a subsequent run and the tails also contain esters which add unique flavors to your whiskey. This is a matter of choice, no right or wrong method.

We will discuss making the cuts between heads, hearts and tails in step 13.

13. Making the Cuts

Making the cuts refers to where in the spirit run you are going to make the divisions between heads, hearts and tails. There are some standard cuts that are used by commercial distillers that can be helpful in deciding where to make your cuts. A guideline you could use as a starting point is called the middle fifth cut used by some commercial distilleries; they use a 75/65 cut. This means everything in a run that is above 75% abv is designated as heads. Everything that is below 65% abv is designated as tails. So everything from 75% to 65% abv is designated as hearts. This is considered to be a very tight cut, thereby producing a very high quality ethanol containing very little heads and very little tails. Of course, if you want more volume, you could use the general commercial distillery cuts of 75/55. For moonshine I prefer **80/60 cuts**. That would be 80% abv and above being heads, below 60% abv being tails. So I keep everything from 79% down to 60% abv as hearts. These are guidelines and will vary some between batches; the ultimate decision is made by smell and taste. The following information will help you make your cuts using the aroma and taste of your distillate. It is helpful to dilute the sample distillate you taste and smell by adding some filtered water. Put a small sample (¼ once) in a glass, add about the same amount of water, smell and taste, spit out the sample, rinse your mouth. Repeat this process until you determine where the cuts should be made. This will take some practice.

Heads
Will have a strong, fruity odor and will have a strong taste with a bite. Contain acetaldehyde, ethyl formate, acetone, methanol, ethyl acetate, and some ethanol.

Hearts
Will smell light and sweet. They will have a smooth sweet taste. Contain primarily ethanol - the good stuff.

Tails
Will smell light a wet dog. They will taste muddy and awful. As soon as the tails start you will be able to smell them in your distillate. Contain fusel oils including propanol, butanol and amyl alcohol. Also contain proteins, carbohydrates, fatty acids, esters and some ethanol.

The skill is being able to sniff out and taste where the heads end and where the tails begin. Use the 75/65 cuts as a guide. Your actual runs may come out a little different than that, but it will give you a starting point. Some of your runs may end up with the heads cut closer to 80% abv and the tails cut closer to 50% abv. They will vary depending on the particular spirit you are making. Making cuts is a skill that takes time to learn.

Be sure to study the spirit run date on the next page, it will enhance your understanding of the process.

The picture below shows the heads cut and tails cut marked in red on the duct tape. All of the jars with an abv of 78% and above will be poured into a separate container and labeled **"heads."** On the other end, all jars with an abv less than 58% will be poured into a separate container and labeled **"tails."** The heads and tails can be kept and added to the next spirit run of the same mash bill. That way you can distill out some more of the ethanol that remains. Some of the heads and tails can also be blended with the hearts to add to the flavor of the final spirit. Blending takes some practice and is based on your own personal tastes. Blend with caution a little at a time.

Each jar has about 4 ounces of distillate. After the run was complete, the heads cut was made at 79% abv and the tails cut at 58% abv. Cuts were based on the aroma and taste of the distillate.

JAR NO.	**TIME**	**TEMP**	**ABV**	**HEAT**	**NOTES**

Moonshine Spirit Run No. 1

JAR NO.	TIME	TEMP	ABV	HEAT	NOTES
---	10:45 am	25°C	---	Medium	
---	11:00 am	55°C	---	Medium	
---	11:05 am	65°C	---	Low	Slow drips
---	11:10 am	70°C	---	Low	"
--	11:15 am	75°C	---	Low	"
---	11:20 am	80°C	---	Low	Fast drips
---	11:25 am	84°C	81%	Low	Removed foreshots, 6 ounces
---	11:25 am	Placed parrot and first spirit jar in place.				
1	11:40 am	84°C	81%	Low	Fast Drips
2	12:00 pm	85°C	80%	Low	Fast Drips
3	12:20 pm	85°C	79%	Low	Heads Cut
4	12:25 pm	85°C	78%	Low	Fast Drips
5	12:25 pm	85°C	77%	Low	Fast Drips
6	12:45 pm	85°C	76%	Low	Fast Drips
7	12:55 pm	87°C	70%	Low	Fast Drips
8	1:10 pm	88°C	70%	Low	Fast Drips

Moonshine Spirit Run No. 1

JAR NO.	TIME	TEMP	ABV	HEAT	NOTES
9	1:20 pm	89°C	69%	Low	Fast Drips
10	1:30 pm	89°C	67%	Low	Fast Drips
11	1:40 pm	90°C	67%	Low	Fast Drips
12	1:50 pm	91°C	64%	Low	Fast Drips
13	2:00 pm	92°C	61%	Low	Fast Drips
14	2:10 pm	93°C	58%	Low	Tails Cut
15	2:20 pm	95°C	51%	Low	Fast Drips
16	2:30 pm	95°C	45%	Low	Fast Drips

- Stopped the run at jar 16. Not interested in distilling out the tails.

- Jars 4 through 14 were kept as hearts.

- Hearts volume: 46 ounces. ABV: 70%   PROOF: 140

- You could keep the hearts for drinking as a lower proof moonshine or distill a third time to get a higher proof. It is up to the distiller to choose.

NOTE:

If you were to proof this batch down to 80 proof (40% abv) you would end up with about three fifths of what would essentially be corn whiskey. If you were to keep it at the higher proof, or distill a third time to increase the proof even further, you would have your moonshine. You would have less volume, but higher proof.

THIRD DISTILLATION
SPIRIT RUN NO. 2

When making moonshine a third distillation may be required to get the desired high proof spirits. Moonshiners would keep track of the distillations of a batch by placing an "X" on a jug for each distillation run. You have probably seen a moonshine jug with three X's indicating three distillations.

When doing a third distillation, follow the steps below.

1. **Pour just the hearts from the first spirit run into your still.**

2. **Add water to dilute the hearts back down to below 40% abv.**

3. **Distill like a normal spirit run.**

4. **Remove foreshots**

Remove 1 ounce per gallon of hearts being distilled. If you had a half gallon of hearts, remove 1/2 ounce of foreshots. Most of the foreshots were removed during the first spirit run, so this is all you need.

5. Continue distilling and filling small mason jars

Collect about 4 ounces per jar. Record temperature and abv for each jar.

6. Distill down to where the tails are prevalent.

7. Make your heads and tails cuts.

Making your cuts from the 2nd spirit run can be a little tricky. The abv may be higher because you are starting with a more purified product. The abv therefore, will not be a reliable method of making your cuts. You will need to rely more on the smell and taste of the distillate to make the cuts. The hearts should have a lightly sweet, almost neutral smell and taste.

AGING YOUR MOONSHINE (If Desired)

Moonshine is <u>not</u> usually aged. However, you can age it if you want to. One method is to place new moonshine in a gallon jar and put three coffee filters on top with a rubber band. Let it sit for a week to allow volatile vapors to escape. I think this improves the smoothness of the moonshine. So, it is sort of aging it a little. After a week, bottle it. You can keep some of your product as moonshine and age some to make corn whiskey if desired. To turn it into whiskey, just proof it down to 125 and age it with oak wood. Commercial whiskey distilleries use charred oak barrels to age their product. Barrels or casks made of American White Oak wood are the most commonly used structures for aging whiskey, although there are some variations to that. Oak barrels are expensive, large (53 gallon), and take years to properly age whiskey. An alternative to barrel aging is jar aging. This requires one-gallon glass jars with lids and either charred or toasted American White Oak cubes. The process is quite simple and will create excellent product in six months or less

First off buy some one-gallon glass jars with lids. You can purchase oak cubes, but they are expensive. It is easy to get some white oak wood, cut it into small pieces and either toast it in an oven or char it with a propane torch. You can char larger amounts by burning it on a camping stove. Proof your spirit down to 125, put it into a jar, place a few oak chunks in, and label your jar. Your oak chunks should be about one-inch square. Technically, by aging your moonshine with wood you are turning it into whiskey. Jar aged whiskey starts to get good after a couple of months, but I recommend letting it age for at least 6 months. After aging proof it down to 80 or whatever you prefer for drinking.

Aging moonshine for a week will improve the smoothness of the product. Three coffee filters fixed to the top of the jar will allow volatile vapors to escape. After a week, bottle it.

If you would like more depth on aging spirits, please check out my other whiskey distilling books at Amazon.com.

Whiskey Distiller's Training Manual
Whiskey Distilling Essentials
Home Distilling Handbook
Home Distilling Handbook, 2nd Edition
The Ultimate Home Distilling Handbook

FILTERING YOUR MOONSHINE

Many commercial distilleries filter their spirits through activated charcoal. Filtering is a matter of personal preference in my opinion. Although filtering will make a spirits smoother, I believe it strips out some of the best flavor congeners. Hence, I don't use charcoal filtering. I do filter my spirits through a coffee filter after aging and that's it. Try filtering and not filtering to see which method you prefer.

BOTTLING YOUR MOONSHINE

You can bottle moonshine immediately after distilling if you wish. I prefer to allow it to settle for a week in a gallon jar before bottling.

1. Proof Down Your to Your Desired Drinking Proof

Decide what proof you want for your moonshine, 160, 90, etc. Measure the volume of moonshine in your jar and measure the abv. Remember that some spirit is always lost due to evaporation during the aging process. Use the dilution calculator at hillbillystills.com/distilling-calculator-s/265.htm. Plug in the numbers and it will tell you how much water to add to your moonshine for the proof you want. Use purified water for proofing down.

2. Rinse Out Your Bottles

3. Filter the Moonshine into Your Bottles

Coffee filters work well for this.

4. Put the Corks in

5. Attach Your Labels

I recommend designing a label on your computer with MS Publisher. Print the label on plain paper. Cut it out and glue it onto your bottle using a glue stick. The glue stick works well and it is easy to remove the label when you need to recycle any bottles. There are also many on-line label printing companies where you can design a custom label and have them produced for you.

MOONSHINE RECIPES

Technically speaking, moonshine is any illegally produced spirit with a high alcohol content. Moonshine per se, is a high-proof, clear, unaged whiskey. Traditional moonshine is made of corn and sugar, or corn and barley malt. The thing to keep in mind is you can make moonshine out of anything you want. I have included a few standard moonshine recipes and some information about creating your own recipes. I recommend aiming for an original gravity of about 1.080 (target gravity) and potential alcohol of about 10%. This would indicate a good sugar content and potential alcohol level, and will not stress your yeast. Excessive sugar content in a mash or an excessive alcohol content in a fermenting wort can stress or even kill your yeast. This can lead to off flavors or a stuck fermentation. Some distillers will go higher than 1.080, but I think it is a safe level that produces a good volume of spirits. If you do cook a mash that goes a little beyond that level it isn't a big deal.

Each of the following moonshine recipes requires 8 gallons of water and 24 pounds of grain, or a combination of grain and sugar. They will make about 10 gallons of mash and produce about 3 fifths of finished product. The higher your proof, the lower your yield will be. A 10 gallon mash will produce about 6 to 7 gallons of fermented wash, just right for the 8 gallon still used as an example in the book. If you have a different size still, simply adjust the recipe as needed, just keep the ratios the same. For each recipe, follow the instructions covered in chapter 5 unless noted otherwise.

Classic Moonshine

Water - 8 Gallons

Corn meal - 80%, 19.2 lb.

Barley malt - 20%, 4.8 lb.

Alpha-amylase enzyme - 1 tsp

Fermax yeast nutrient - 10 tsp

Yeast - 5 tsp

(if you use a different nutrient, following the package instructions)

Distill 3 times per instructions on page 94.

Keep high proof.

Do not age.

Popcorn Sutton's Moonshine

Water - 8 gallons

Corn meal - 5 lb.

Malted grain (barley, corn, or rye) - 7 lb. [source of enzymes]

Sugar - 10 lb.

Yeast - 5 tsp

Directions - specifically for this recipe
1. Add 2 gallons of water to the pot and bring it to boil.
2. Add cornmeal, cook at 165 °F. Mix well.
3. Remove the heat and let the cornmeal cool down to 150°F.
4. Once cooled to 150 °F add the remaining water, then mix in the sugar and ground malt grain.
5. Let it cool to about 80 °F.
6. Add yeast, mix well.
7. Aerate.
8. Transfer mixture into the fermenter with mash bag inserted.
9. Put lid on the fermenter. Using an airlock lid is optional.

10. Allow to ferment for 5 - 7 days. SG should be down to close to 1.000 when complete.
11. Remove wash and distill per instructions in chapter 5.

Sugar Shine

Water - 8 Gallons

Sugar - 16 lb.

Fermax nutrient - 10 tsp

Yeast - 5 tsp

Corn and Sugar Moonshine

Water - 8 Gallons

Corn, flaked or meal - 70%, 16.8 lb.

Barley malt - 10%, 2.4 lb.

Sugar - 20%, 4.8 lb.

Amylase enzyme - 1 tsp

Fermax Nutrient - 10 tsp

Yeast - 5 tsp

Barley Moonshine

Water - 8 Gallons

Barley malt - 15%, 24 lb.

Barley - 85%, 20.4 lb.

Amylase enzyme - 1 tsp

Fermax yeast nutrient - 10 tsp

Yeast - 5 tsp

Sweet Feed Moonshine

It is sold at feed stores. Also called wet COB.

Water - 8 Gallons

Sweet feed - 85%, 20.4 lb.

Barley Malt - 15%, 3.6 lb.

Amylase enzyme - 1 tsp

Fermax yeast nutrient - 10 tsp

Yeast - 5 tsp

Oat Moonshine

Water - 8 Gallons

Oats - rolled or flaked - 80%, 19.2 lb.

Barley Malt - 20%, 4.8 lb.

Amylase enzyme - 1 tsp

Fermax yeast nutrient - 10 tsp

Yeast - 5 tsp

Barley Malt Moonshine

Water - 8 Gallons

Barley Malt - 19.2 lb.

Sugar - 4.8 lb.

Amylase enzyme - 1 tsp

Fermax yeast nutrient - 10 tsp

Yeast - 5 tsp

Grandpa's Oat Moonshine

Adapted from: advancedmixology.com

Water - 6 gallons

Sugar - 10 lb.

Quick oats - 2½ lb.

Brown sugar - 2 lb.

Pomelo fruit - 1 ripe, peeled and chopped

Fermax yeast nutrient - 6 tsp

Yeast - 4 tsp

Cracked Corn Moonshine

You may have noticed that cracked corn has a lower specific gravity when mashed than either flaked corn or corn meal. It comes in at about 1.030. Cracked corn needs to be ground finer in order to expose more of the starch. I use a grain grinder and run cracked corn through it twice. I also find that allowing the cracked corn to rest longer in the cooking pot during mashing will help in the saccharification process and produce a higher OG.

Water - 8 gallons

Cracked Corn - 10 lb.

Sugar - 10 lb.

Amylase enzyme - 1 tsp

Fermax yeast nutrient - 10 tsp

Yeast - 5 tsp

DEVELOPING YOUR OWN MOONSHINE RECIPES

You can make moonshine out of any grains, fruits, vegetables, or sources of sugar you want, but how do you know if your recipes will work? There are some easy calculations you can make that will answer that question for any recipe you create. First, we need to cover some basics that will help you determine the efficacy of the recipes you develop.

Mash Volume

Mash volume includes all of the water and ingredients you add to a recipe. You will need to know how much your mash volume will increase when you add different ingredients. Knowing the total mash volume (TMV) is needed when calculating the expected sugar content, expected potential alcohol of a recipe, and to determine if the mash will fit your equipment.

Volume Added by Grain: Approximately .08 gallons per pound of grain. For example, 20 pounds of grain will add about 1.6 gallons to TMV. $20 \times .08 = 1.6$

Volume Added by Sugar: Approximately 18.28 ounces of volume per pound of sugar. 7 pounds of sugar adds about 1 gallon of volume.

Mash Efficiency

Mash efficiency (ME) is the percentage of the starches in a grain actually converted to sugar during the mashing process. You will not get 100% ME. The average ME is about 80%. This is also know as conversion.

To calculate the expected original gravity and expected potential alcohol for a particular grain recipe you will need to use the "Specific Gravity for Grains and Sugars" chart on page 142. For fruit recipes use the "Fruit Juice Specific Gravity" chart on page 143. In these charts, specific gravity is shown for each item. For example, corn meal has a SG of 1.037. That is the SG of 1 pound of corn meal in 1 gallon of water. So corn meal, in water, has a higher density than water which has a SG of 1.000. The specific gravity is measuring the amount of sugar in the solution. The 1.037 SG for corn meal is also known as 37 gravity points per gallon or 37 PPG. Knowing the total gravity points of a mash allows us to estimate the expected potential alcohol that could be produced by fermenting the mash or the wort from the mash. Like I mentioned earlier, I like to aim for a 10% PA in my mash recipes; 10% is my target PA. They don't have to be exactly 10%, just in that area. Knowing the gravity points contributed by each item in a recipe allows us to determine the total gravity points so we can see if the recipe will actually work. Take a look at the following example.

Classic Moonshine Recipe - Will it Work?

We need to determine if this recipe will produce the sugar we need for a successful fermentation and ultimately produce a reasonable quantity of distillate.

Water - 8 gallons
Corn meal - 19.2 lb.
Barley Malt - 4.8 lb.

Start by calculating the gravity points using the chart on page 142.

Gravity Points

Corn meal: 37 X 19.2 lb. = 710.4

Barley Malt: 37 X 4.8 lb. = 177.6

Total Gravity Points: = 888

888 X .80 (ME) = 710.4/10 (TMV) = 1.071 OG, 9.2% PA

This is pretty close to our 10% PA target so it will work out fine. We could add some sugar if we wanted to bump it up a bit, but not really necessary.

You can preform this calculation for any recipe you want to try. Then you will not waste your time and money on a recipe that won't produce a decent amount of product.

ADDING SUGAR TO A RECIPE

Sometimes you may need, or want, to add some sugar to a recipe to increase the SG and PA. There is a simple way to do that using the chart on page 144.

For an example, suppose you produce a mash that ends up with an SG and PA lower than you want. You can add sugar, but you don't want to go overboard. Too much sugar will reduce the flavor of your spirit and can have harmful affects on your yeast. I recommend shooting for a SG of 1.080 which is a PA of 10.5%; between 8 and 12% PA is good. Follow the instructions below when adding sugar. Refer to the chart on page 144.

Let's say you prepare a 10 gallon moonshine mash and your original gravity (OG) is 1.050 for a PA of 6.6%, but you want a PA of about 10%. Calculate the required sugar as follows:

From the chart, OG of 1.050 equates to 21 ounces of sugar per gallon of mash.

Desired OG of 1.080 (10.5% PA) equates to 33 ounces of sugar per gallon of mash.

33 - 21 = 12 ounces per gallon of mash needed.

12 X 10 gal. mash = 120 ounces (7.5 pounds) of sugar needed.

Add 7.5 pounds of sugar, mix it in, recheck your gravity.

DISTILLING SAFETY

Distilling spirits is actually very safe if common sense is applied. Here are some of the critical items to keep in mind when distilling.

1. DO NOT LEAVE YOUR STILL UNATTENDED.

2. AN ELECTRIC HOT PLATE IS THE SAFEST WAY TO HEAT YOUR STILL.

3. A PROPANE BURNER CAN BE USED WITH PROPER PRE-CAUTIONS.

4. KEEP YOUR CONDENSER WATER COOL.

5. HIGH PROOF ALCOHOL AND VAPOR ARE VERY FLAMMABLE.

6. DO NOT FILL YOUR STILL MORE THAN 3/4 FULL.

7. DISCARD THE FORESHOTS - THEY CONTAIN METHA NOL.

8. KEEP A FIRE EXTINGUISHER NEARBY.

9. SEAL ALL LEAKS IN YOUR SYSTEM WITH FLOUR PASTE.

10. MAKE SURE TO HAVE GOOD VENTILATION.

11. USE GLASS DISTILLATE COLLECTION JARS - NEVER PLASTIC.

12. DIRECT THE DISTILLATE AWAY FROM YOUR STILL.

Expanded Glossary

Adjuncts

Unmalted grains added to the mash.

Aerate

To introduce air and oxygen into something. Introducing air into the wort, for example.

Alcohols and other Compounds in the Distillate

There are a number of different alcohols and compounds produced by the yeast during fermentation. When we distill the wash the different alcohols and compounds will boil and vaporize at different temperatures. The table below shows the different products that may be distilled out of a typical wash and the temperature at which each will boil. These are the temperatures at which each product will boil if the solution is made of 100% of that particular product. For example, if we had a container with 100% pure ethanol in it, it would boil and 78.4°C. When we have a typical wash containing different fractions of each product, the actual boiling points will be higher due to the fact that they are not in a 100% pure state; they are diluted in water. The boiling points are used as a guide to help determine when each product is vaporized during distillation. See the chart on the net page.

112

Alcohols and other Compounds in the Distillate

Product	Formula	Temp.
Acetaldehyde	C_2H_4O	20.2°C (68.4°F)
Ethyl Formate	$C_3H_6O_2$	54.3°C (129.7°F)
Acetone	C_3H_6O	56.0°C (132.8°F)
Methanol - Wood Alcohol	CH_3OH	64.7°C (148.5°F)
Ethyl Acetate	$C_4H_8O_2$	77.1°C (170.8°F)
Ethanol	C_2H_6O	78.4°C (173.1°F)
2-Propanol	C_3H_8O	82.6°C (180.7°F)
1-Propanol - Rubbing alcohol	C_3H_8O	97.0°C (206.6°F)
Water	H_2O	100.0°C (212°F)
Butanol	$C_4H_{10}O$	117.7°C (243.9°F)
Acetic Acid	CH_3COOH	118.1°C (244.6°F)
Amyl Alcohol	$C_5H_{12}O$	131.6°C (268.9°F)
Furfural	$C_5H_4O_2$	161.7°C (323.1°F)

Alcohol By Volume (ABV)

Alcohol By Volume is usually abbreviated as ABV. It is the concentration of total alcohol, as a percentage, in the distillate or in a bottle of spirits.

For example, 40% ABV.

Alpha-Amylase Enzyme

Alpha-amylase enzyme is an enzyme produced by germinating seeds or grain like barley. The enzyme helps break down long chained sugars (starch) into smaller carbohydrates containing one, two, or three glucose molecules. These can then be fermented by the yeast. The picture below illustrates the structure of a starch molecule. The enzyme breaks the bonds in between the glucose molecules.

Alcohol Hydrometer (Alcoholometer)

Hydrometer used to measure the alcohol content of a solution. The tool shows the alcohol by volume (abv), as a percentage, as well as the proof of the solution. Proof is two times the abv.

Alcohol Parrot

A copper tube that receives distillate from a still condenser and holds an alcohol hydrometer. This allows the distiller to see real-time abv readings as the distillation proceeds.

Amylopectin

A water-insoluble polysaccharide and highly branched polymer of α-glucose units found in plants. It is one of the two components of starch, the other being amylose.

Amylose

Amylose is a polysaccharide made of α-D-glucose units bonded to each other through α glycosidic bonds. Amylose is a straight linear chain of glucose molecules linked by α-1,4 glycosidic linkages It is one of the two components of starch, making up approximately 20-30%.

Angel's Share

The spirit lost to evaporation out of the oak barrels during aging. About 2% of the spirits are lost to evaporation each year.

Attenuation

The decline in the specific gravity of the wort as the yeast converts sugars to alcohol. Can also be expressed as the percentage of sugars the yeast consumes during fermentation, normally from 65 to 80%.

Auto Siphon

A convenient tool for removing wash from a fermenter and backset from a still.

Back Set

The wash left at the end of a stripping run that can be added into the next batch of mash. Normally used to replace 25% of the water needed in a new batch of mash. This creates a sour mash and acidifies (lowers the pH) the mash.

Bacteria

Bacteria are microscopic single-celled organisms. There are many kinds of bacteria, some are harmful, but many are beneficial. There are several species of Lactobacillus bacteria that can enter your mash naturally or can be added intentionally. Lactobacillus will produce various acids that are used in the creation of esters in the wort. The esters will have a flavorful effect on your whiskey. You can purchase Lactobacillus bacteria to incorporate into your mash if desired.

Baking Soda

Sodium bicarbonate, $NaHCO_3$. Used to raise pH.

Barm

The foam formed on the top of a fermenting liquid or mash.

Base Malt

Base malts make up part of the grist in an all-grain mash. If you are making a bourbon for example, barley malt would be the base malt to which other grains are added.

Beta-Amylase Enzyme

Beta-amylase is an enzyme also produced by germinating seeds or grains. The enzyme breaks chemical bonds at the end of the sugar chains (starch). This process produces two-chained sugars like maltose. It is an important process in whiskey making because is helps facilitate the saccharification process.

Blending

The process of carefully adding heads and or tails to a batch of hearts in order to attain a certain flavor in the final whiskey product. This takes a fair amount of skill to do correctly.

Boiling

Heating a liquid to the temperature at which it bubbles and turns to vapor. Boiling occurs below the surface of a heated liquid. Ethanol boils in relation to its concentration in water. The lower the concentration of ethanol in water, the higher the boiling temperature of the ethanol.

Bottled in Bond

A label for an American-made distilled beverage that has been aged and bottled according to a set of legal regulations contained in the United States government's Standards of Identity for Distilled Spirits, as originally laid out in the Bottled-in-Bond Act of 1897.

Carbohydrate

The main types of carbohydrates are monosaccharides, disaccharides, and polysaccharides. Carbohydrates consist of molecules of glucose bonded together. Glucose molecules are composed of carbon, hydrogen, and oxygen atoms in the chemical structure of $C_6H_{12}O_6$. Glucose is also known as a simple sugar or monosaccharide. It is the primary source of energy for living things including the yeast we rely on for fermentation.

Charge

The charge is the amount of liquid, e.g., low wines, being placed in a still for distillation.

Citric Acid, $HOC(CH_2CO_2H)_2$

Citric acid is an organic compound. It is a colorless weak organic acid. It occurs naturally in citrus fruits. Citric acid can be used to increase the acidity of a mash. Many of the enzymes that break down the starches in a mash function best at lower pH levels. Using citric acid can help lower the mash pH level to increase the starch conversion rate.

Congeners

Congeners are substances other than ethanol that are produced during fermentation. They can effect the flavor of the distillate positively or negatively.

Copper Sulfate ($CuSO_4$)

When distilling with a copper still, sulfur, produced by the yeast during fermentation, binds with the copper to produce copper sulfate. This is good because it removes the sulfur from your distillate. When you clean your still the copper sulfate is washed away.

Cuts

During distillation the cuts are the points at which the distiller separates the heads and the tails leaving the hearts of the run.

Cutting

Diluting an alcohol spirit by adding water. Also known as proofing down.

DADY (Distiller's Active Dry Yeast)

DADY is a good all-purpose yeast that is good for making whiskey and other spirits.

Dephlegmator (duh-fleg-mater)

Also known as a reflux condenser, a dephlegmator is located at the top of a column still. Its purpose is to condense vapors back into liquid and send them back down the column into the still where they are re-vaporized (reflux). This creates a purer distillate.

Dextrin

A type of starch made from mixtures of polymers of D-glucose molecules. Produced by breaking apart starch or glycogen.

Dextrinase

An enzyme in malted grain that cleaves the alpha-1,6 linkage in dextrins to produce glucose.

Diacetyl $(CH_3CO)_2$

A yellow or green liquid with an intensely buttery flavor. Diacetyl is a by-product produced by yeast during fermentation and occurs naturally in alcoholic beverages.

Diammonium Phosphate (DAP)

DAP is a pure form of yeast nutrient containing nitrogen and phosphorus. Use ½ tsp per 5 gallons of mash. Not needed in all grain mashes.

Distillate

The liquid produced from the process of distillation. In our case, ethanol plus other forms of alcohol.

Enzyme

A protein that acts as a biological catalyst. Catalysts accelerate chemical reactions. Acts upon a substrate and produces a product.

Enzyme Conversion

Enzymes are compounds responsible for converting starches in a mash into fermentable sugars.

Esters

Esters are compounds produced during fermentation. They result from the combination of alcohols and fatty acids or acetates. Esters add aromas and flavors to the spirit.

Important Esters in Distilling	Flavor
Butyl Acetate	Apple
Ethyl Acetate	Pear
Ethyl Butyrate	Pineapple
Ethyl Cinnamate	Cinnamon
Ethyl Hexanoate	Apple
Isoamyl Acetate	Banana
Methyl Trans-Cinnamate	Strawberry
Octyl Acetate	Orange
Propyl Acetate	Pear

Esterification

A reaction of an alcohol with an acid to produce an ester and water.

Ethanol (C_2H_5OH)

Ethanol, also known as ethyl alcohol, is one of the alcohols produced by yeast during sugar fermentation. It has a specific gravity of 0.789, less dense and lighter than water.

Evaporation

Evaporation occurs at the surface of a boiling liquid as the liquid transitions into vapor.

Exogenous Enzyme

Enzymes that are supplied from an external source, not naturally found in the grains or other carbohydrate sources being mashed.

Extraction Efficiency

AKA Mash Efficiency. The amount of fermentable sugar actually produced from a mash. An average mash efficiency for grains is 75%.

FAN (Free Amino Nitrogen)

The concentration of individual amino acids and small peptides (one to three units) which can be utilized by yeast for cell growth and re-production during fermentation. |

Feints

The final distillate from a spirit run. The feints are low in alcohol and can be added to the next run and redistilled.

Felting

Felting is a condition where the grain roots grow together during the malting process. It is not a desirable situation. It makes it had to separate the grains before drying and further processing.

Fermentation

Fermentation is the process of converting sugars, like glucose and maltose, into acids, carbon dioxide (CO_2), and various alcohols by yeasts. The breakdown of glucose also releases carbon atoms which can be used by the yeast to grow and reproduce (budding). It is important to make sure the yeasts have an ample supply of oxygen and other nutrients at the beginning of their life cycle for efficient fermentation.

Fermenter

AKA Fermentation bucket, a fermenter is a container that wort or wash is poured or siphoned into after cooling to facilitate fermentation.

Ferment Off The Grain

The wort is separated from the mash and fermented.

Ferment On The Grain

The entire mash, including grains and wort, is fermented.

Flocculation

Yeasts' ability to clump together and settle out at the end of a fermentation. They are dormant at this stage, not dead.

Foreshots

The first few ounces of distillate produced during a distillation. They contain methanol and other volatile alcohols.

Fructose ($C_6H_{12}O_6$)

Fructose (Frook - tose) is a simple sugar that is a polymer of glucose. It has the exact same chemical formula as glucose, just arranged differently.

Fructophilic

Prefers to ferment fructose. Some yeast strains will ferment fructose first, then glucose. They are fructophilic.

Fusel Oils

Fusel oils are higher order alcohols. Fusel is a German word which means "bad liquor." They have an oily consistency, smell like a wet dog, and taste bad. Fusel oils include: propanol, butanol, amyl alcohol, and furfural.

Gelatinization

When using corn meal or polenta as your source of corn in a batch, the corn must first be gelatinized. This involves heating the corn in water which breaks the bonds between the starch molecules. This basically dissolves the starch and allows the corn to absorb more water. The mixture will become very thick. Once the corn is gelatinized you can add the remaining grains (e.g., barley malt, rye) and proceed to cook the batch.

Glucoamylase

Glucoamylase is a fungal-derived enzyme which breaks down dextrins into simple sugars.

Glucose ($C_6H_{12}O_6$)

A simple sugar which is an important energy source in living organisms and is a component of many carbohydrates.

Glucophilic

Prefers to ferment glucose. Some yeast strains prefer to ferment glucose first. They are glucophilic.

Glycogen ($C_{24}H_{42}O_{21}$)

Glycogen is a multibranched polysaccharide of glucose that serves as a form of energy storage in animals, fungi, and bacteria. The polysaccharide structure represents the main storage form of glucose in the body.

Glycolysis

The breakdown of glucose by enzymes, releasing energy and pyruvic acid.

Grain Bill

In the distilling industry the grain bill is simply a list of which grains are used to make the mash and the percentage of each. For example, the grain bill for Jack Daniels Tennessee Whiskey is 80% corn, 12% rye and 8% malted barley. Of course, trying to make Jack Daniels whiskey isn't just a matter of using their grain bill. They use various techniques in their production process that produces the unique flavors of Jack Daniels, techniques that are closely guarded secrets.

Grain Cap

The layer of grain pushed up by carbon dioxide produced by yeast during fermentation. You will see a grain cap form at the top of your fermenter.

Gravity

Refers to specific gravity. The total amount of dissolved solids in water; usually referring to dissolved sugars.

Gravity Unit

Specific gravity of different mash ingredients can be shown as gravity units. For example, the specific gravity of one pound of flaked corn in one gallon of water is 1.037. This would be 37 gravity units. It is usually expressed as the **PPG (Points Per Pound Per Gallon).** Gravity units are used to calculate the total original gravity (OG) of a mash or wort.

Grist

Ground grain.

Gypsum

Calcium sulfate, $CaSO_4$. Used to lower pH.

Heads

The first major part of the distillate is called the heads. The heads contain compounds like acetone, acetaldehyde, acetate and some ethanol. They have a strong, almost fruity smell and taste harsh. Heads can be discarded or collected and added to the next spirit run. Approximately 20-30% of the liquid collected during a distillation run will be heads.

Hearts

The hearts contain mainly ethanol and are the part of the spirit run we want to collect and make into whiskey. Hearts will have a light sweet smell and a light sweet, smooth taste. The skill of the distiller is in developing the ability to smell and taste the different fractions of distillate in order to separate the heads, hearts and tails effectively. Approximately 30-40% of the run will be hearts. See Appendix A for an illustration of Heads, Hearts and Tails.

Hydrolysis

Hydrolysis is any chemical reaction in which a molecule of water breaks one or more chemical bonds causing a larger molecule to be broken into smaller molecules.

Infusion Mash

A mashing technique where hot brewing water is blended with malts to create a mash that only has one rest, at saccharification temperature.

Iodine Starch Test

Used to test for the presence of starch in a solution. Place a few drops of wort on a plate. Place a few drops of iodine into the wort and mix together. If it turns blue/black there is still starch that has not been converted to fermentable sugars.

Kraeusen

Foamy head that forms on top of fermenting wort after about 4 hours of fermentation. Consists of dead yeast and proteins.

Lactic Acid ($C_3H_6O_3$)

Lactic acid is an organic acid. It can be used to reduce alkalinity (lower pH) in mash. The lactic acid used is food grade and made by fermentation of natural beet or cane sugar.

Lautering

To rinse off and separate the wort from the mash. Lauter comes from the German word abläutern, meaning to rinse off or purify.

Lees

The layer of dormant yeast that accumulate in the bottom of the fermenter or vat.

Liebig Condenser

A Liebig condenser is a straight condenser consisting of a single tube within a larger tube or water jacket. It is used to cool and condense a gas/vapor back to a liquid. It is often used as a primary condenser for distilling alcoholic spirits.

Lime

Calcium carbonate, $CaCO_3$ Used to raise pH.

Low Wines

The distillate produced from the first distillation (stripping run) of a fermented wash. Usually have an abv of about 40%.

Lyne Arm

The tube going from the still head to the condenser.

Malt

Any germinated cereal grain that has been dried with hot air in order to halt germination. Known as "malting."

Malt Extract

A sweet, treacle like syrup, made from malted barley. Used in brewing.

Maceration

To soften and break down organic tissue, e.g., fruits, by exposure to moisture.

Maltase

An enzyme in barley that hydrolyzes (breaks down) maltose into glucose.

Maltose

Maltose, also known as maltobiose or malt sugar, is a disaccharide formed from two units of glucose joined with an α bond.

Mash

Cooked mixture of grains and water.

Mash Bill

The mix of grains being used to make a spirit.

Mashing

The process of extracting starches from grains with water and enzymatically converting them into fermentable sugars yeast can use.

Mash Bag

A net-like bag used to cook or ferment mash in. The bag makes it easy to remove the grain and separate out the wort from the mash.

Mash Efficiency

AKA Extraction Efficiency. The amount of fermentable sugar actually produced from the starches in a mash. An average mash efficiency for grains is 75%.

Mash Tun

A vessel used for mixing ground grains (grist) with temperature-controlled water.

Neutral Based Spirit

Non-flavored alcohol of 95% abv obtained chiefly from grain or molasses.

Miscible

Liquids that can form a homogeneous mixture when added together.

New Make Spirit

New make is unaged whiskey. The clear liquid that comes off the still at about 70% abv and before it's moved into a barrel. It is most commonly associated with Scotch, but new make can be any style of whiskey.

Open Fermentation

Fermentations that take place in vessels that are open to the environment.

Original Gravity (OG)

The starting specific gravity of a wort before fermentation indicating the amount of sugar present. Can be used to determine the potential alcohol of the wort.

Oxidation

Oxidation occurs when an atom, molecule, or ion loses one or more electrons in a chemical reaction. Oxidation doesn't necessarily involve oxygen, but sometimes it does. Originally, the term was used when oxygen caused electron loss in a reaction.

Pasteurization

Pasteurization is the process of heating, juice, wine, beer, and other liquid foods to kill yeast, bacteria, and other pathogens. Heat to 71°C (160°F) for 1 minute.

pH

Potential hydrogen. pH measures the acidity and alkalinity of a substance. We are concerned about the pH of our mash and our wort prior to fermentation. The pH scale is a logarithmic scale that goes from 0 to 14. Seven is neutral, anything below 7 is acidic, and anything above 7 is alkaline. Acidic substances have a high concentration of hydrogen ions (H^+) and alkaline substances have a high concentration of hydroxyl ions (OH^-).

In the distilling business the optimum pH for mash is between 5.2 and 5.7, moderately acidic. This pH range improves the activity of the enzymes responsible for saccharification and gives us a better conversion of the starches in the mash to glucose. It is a good idea to check the pH of your mash with a pH test strip or a digital pH meter. The good news is that mash is naturally in the pH range of 5.2 to 5.7 because grains are acidic by nature.

The optimum pH for fermentation by the yeast is between 4.0 and 4.5. Yeast thrive in a acidic environment and are the most healthy in this pH range. This pH also helps control bacterial growth.

You should check the pH of your wort prior to fermentation. If the pH values for either your mash of your wort are high or low you can adjust them quiet easily. For a pH that is too low, too acidic, you can add calcium carbonate (lime). Mix in 1/2 tsp at a time. Recheck your pH. Keep adding 1/2 tsp at a time until you get it into the correct range. For a pH that is to high, too alkaline, add citric acid or calcium sulfate (gypsum). Mix in 1/2 tsp at a time. Recheck your pH. Keep adding 1/2 tsp at a time until you get it into the correct range. When you check your pH levels you might find they are fine. However, there are variables that can cause your pH to be out of the correct range, one of which is your water.

Pitching Yeast

Putting yeast into the mash or the wort.

Polishing

Filtering the distillate to remove congeners. An activated carbon filter is normally used. Also removes flavor.

PPG

Points Per Pound Per Gallon. The number of specific gravity points per pound of ingredient in a gallon of water. For example, a specific gravity of 1.080 would be 80 gravity points.

Polysaccharide

Polysaccharides, or polycarbohydrates, are the most abundant carbohydrates found in food, including grains. They are long chain polymeric carbohydrates composed of monosaccharide units, like glucose, bound together by glycosidic linkages. Often referred to as complex carbohydrates, polysaccharides can react with water using amylase enzymes as a catalyst, which breaks the polysaccharides apart to yield individual glucose molecules.

Potential Alcohol (PA)

This is the amount of alcohol we would expect to be produced from the fermentation of the wort. Most batches of wort will have between 8 and 10% potential alcohol.

Proof

Alcohol proof is twice the percentage of alcohol by volume. So if you have a whiskey that is 40% abv it would be 80 proof.

Primary Condenser

A primary condenser is the main condenser being used during a distillation. The condenser cools alcohol vapors back into liquid as the vapors pass through the condenser. A pot still setup typically used a worm condenser, where a column still uses a shell and tube condenser.

Protease

An enzyme that breaks down proteins into amino acids.

Racking

Moving wash from one vessel to another.

Rectification

The process of repeated distillation that produces a purified product. The product being ethanol in the case of spirit distillation.

Saccharification

The breaking apart of polysaccharides (complex sugars and starches) to soluble sugars like glucose is called saccharification. Malted barley containing beta-amylase enzyme, and the addition of alpha-amylase enzyme to the mash, break the starch molecules in the grains apart to produce single molecules of glucose (simple sugar). The glucose can then be consumed by the yeast during fermentation.

Shotgun Condenser

A shotgun condenser is a type of primary condenser that has multiple tubes, usually from 3 to 7, inside a main outer tube. Whereas a Liebig condenser has a single tube within the main outer tube.

Single Barrel

Single barrel whiskey (or single cask whisky), is whiskey that comes from an individual aging barrel, instead of being created by blending together the contents of different barrels.

Single Malt Scotch

Single malt whisky made at a single distillery in Scotland.

Small Batch Whiskey

Small batch whiskey is whiskey that is produced by mixing the contents of a small number of selected barrels. So, it is blended whiskey.

Soluble

A substance able to be dissolved, especially in water.

Sour Mash

Sour mash whiskey is made by adding some backset or spent mash from a previous batch to the mash of a new batch. Sour mash is typically made with backset contributing 25% of the total liquid in a mash. In the case of using spent mash, about 5 pounds is added to a 10 gallon mash. The mash becomes "sour" from the growth of Lactobacillus bacteria. The bacteria produces lactic acid which lowers the pH of the mash, known as acidification. This keeps other bacteria from growing in, and ruining, the mash. Ensuring the proper mash pH helps to control bacteria like Clostridium butyricum which can ruin the batch. The use of sour mash can create a fuller flavor profile in the finished product and help maintain a more consistent flavor between batches.

Sparging

Sparging is a step at the end of the mashing process where hot water, 170°F (77°C), is run through the grain bed to extract more of the sugar from the grain.

Specific Gravity (SG)

In technical terms, the density of a substance divided by the density of the water. In distilling the substance would be sugar or alcohol. For example, the density of sugar divided by the density of water.

Specialty Malt

Specialty malts are malted grains that vary based on processing and grain type. They undergo the same malting processes as other malts but have experienced different heat and moisture treatments designed to produce different flavor and color. Roasting is a common treatment.

Spelt (Triticum spelta)

Spelt is an ancient species of wheat that was cultivated as far back as 5000 BC. The grain is still grown in some countries.

Spirit

From Aristotle, in 327 B.C., who thought drinking distilled beer or wine put spirit into the body of the drinker.

Starch

AKA amylum. Starch is a polymeric (consisting of many units bonded together) carbohydrate consisting of numerous glucose units joined by glycosidic bonds. This polysaccharide (complex sugar) is produced by most green plants for energy storage. The two main components of starch are amylose (10-20%), and amylopectin (80-90%).

Sugar Hydrometer (Saccharometer)

Hydrometer that measures the specific gravity of a solution; the wort and/or wash in the case of whiskey production. This shows the amount of sugar in the solution which can be used to indicate the potential alcohol.

Tails

The tails occur at the end of the run. Tails do contain some ethanol as well as fusel oils like propanol, butanol and amyl alcohol. Tails also contain water, carbohydrates and proteins. You will know when the tails start because they smell like a wet dog and taste muddy. You will also see an oily sheen on top of the distillate as the tails continue to distill and the distillate will start to look cloudy. Tails can be discarded or collected and added to the next spirit run. Tails will make up approximately 20-30% of a spirit run.

Terminal Gravity (TG)

Also called final gravity, terminal gravity is the specific gravity of a wort at the end of fermentation. Ideally about 1.000.

Torrified

A process of treating wheat with a high-temperature heat treatment that breaks down the cellular structure of the grain. The torrefied wheat is now pre-gelatinized, so you just need to crush or flake it before adding it to the mash. Produces a wheat that adds a neutral flavor to alcoholic beverages.

Trub

Pronounced "troob", it is the sediment at the bottom of the fermenter that comprises all the unfermentable products in wort such as fats, proteins, dormant and dead yeast. The yeast layer is known separately as the lees and is part of the trub.

Volatile

A substance that quickly and easily evaporates at normal temperatures.

Vorlauf

A German word for recirculation. The process of pouring heated wort back into the grain bed for sparging.

Wash

The wash is the liquid produced after fermentation is completed. It will normally contain 8 to 10% alcohol. The wash goes into the still for distillation. Wash also refers to the liquid prepared from juice or sugar based products which will be fermented and distilled.

White Dog

The alcohol that comes out of the still and is placed into aging barrels is called white dog. It has no color and little whiskey flavor at this point. It is the raw distillate. White dog is similar to vodka except that it is made only from grains and is distilled at a lower proof than vodka.

Wort

The wort is the liquid produced from the mashing process. It contains glucose which will be fermented by yeast. By using a sugar hydrometer we can measure the specific gravity of the wort and determine what is known as the potential alcohol level.

Wort Chiller

A device made of copper or stainless steel tubing used to cool wort prior to fermentation. The tube is placed into a container of heated wort. A cold water source is connected to the tube. Water flows through the tube and cools the wort.

YAN

Yeast Assimilable Nitrogen. Nitrogen sources that can be used by yeast. Including Free ammonia nitrogen, Ammonia (NH_3), and Ammonium (NH_4).

Yeast

Yeasts are microorganisms that ferment the wort and create alcohol. They are single celled microorganisms classified as members of the fungi kingdom. Saccharomyces cerevisiae is the primary species of yeast used in the distillation of spirits, however, there are many strains of yeast used within that species by the different distilleries. I recommend Distiller's Active Dry Yeast (DADY). This is a good all purpose yeast for distilling that works very well. Once you become an experienced distiller you can branch out and try different strains. Adding yeast to the mash is called "pitching" the yeast. Keep your yeast in an airtight container in the refrigerator.

Yeast Autolysis

Yeast autolysis is the breaking open or rupturing of the yeast cell and the transfer (leaking out) of undesirable substances and off-flavors into the wash. Yeast autolysis is caused by any conditions that stress the yeast during fermentation.

Yeast Energizer

Yeast energizers contain components such as diammonium phosphate, yeast hulls, magnesium sulfate, vitamin B complexes and tricalcium phosphate. Energizers are used to give a boost to a fermentation that is sluggish or stuck during the fermentation process.

Yeast Nutrients

The source of energy consumed by yeast is glucose, but yeast also requires other nutrients in order to reproduce and grow. Yeast nutrient blends contain a mix of trace elements, inorganic nitrogen, organic nitrogen, zinc and phosphates that helps yeast grow and complete fermentation. Yeast nutrients are added to the mash at the same time as the yeast is pitched.

Yeast Starter

To make a yeast starter get a cup of warm water, 43°C (110°F), add 1 tsp of sugar. Mix in the required amount of yeast. Allow it to sit for about 15 minutes, or until you see a good head of foam (barm) forming on top. Then add it to your mash. This rehydrates the yeast and gets it going well before you pitch it. It is a good way to make sure your have viable yeast.

Yogurt

Some distillers use plain yogurt or other sources of Lactobacillus bacteria in their mash recipes. It is believed that Lactobacillus will produce various acids that will be made into esters by the yeast during fermentation. These esters have a positive impact on the flavor of the spirits. Lactobacillus will also help keep bad bacteria from growing in your mash. You can experiment with this.

Charts

ABV TEMPERATURE CORRECTION

Temp ºF	0-25 Proof	25-50 Proof	50-200 Proof
100	-14	-12	-16
95	-12	-10.5	-14
90	-10	-9	-12
85	-8.5	-7.5	-10
80	-7	-6	-8
75	-5	-4.5	-6
70	-3	-3	-4
65	-1.5	-1.5	-2
60	0	0	0
55	+1.5	+1.5	+2
50	+3.5	+3	+4
45	+5	+4.5	+6
40	+7	+6	+8
35	+9	+8	+10
30	+10.5	+9	+12
25	+12	+10.5	+14
20	+14	+12	+16
15	+16	+13.5	+18
10	+18	+15	+20
5	+19	+16.5	+22
0	+21	+18	+24

SPECIFIC GRAVITY & POTENTIAL ALCOHOL

Specific Gravity (20ºC/68ºF)	Potential Alcohol (%/Volume)
1.000	0.0
1.005	0.7
1.010	1.3
1.015	2.0
1.020	2.6
1.025	3.3
1.030	4.0
1.035	4.6
1.040	5.3
1.045	5.9
1.050	6.6
1.055	7.2
1.060	7.9
1.065	8.6
1.070	9.2
1.075	9.9
1.080	10.5
1.085	11.2
1.090	11.8
1.095	12.5
1.100	13.2
1.110	14.0

Specific Gravity for Grains and Sugars

ITEM	SPECIFIC GRAVITY
Barley	1.040
Barley Malt - 2 row	1.037
Barley – Flaked	1.032
Barley – Peated	1.034
Barley – Raw	1.028
Chocolate Barley Malt	1.028
Corn - Cracked Feed Corn	1.030
Corn – Flaked	1.037
Corn – Meal	1.037
Honey	1.032
Maple syrup	1.030
Molasses	1.036
Oats – Flaked	1.037
Oats – Rolled	1.025
Rice – Flaked	1.032
Rye – Flaked	1.036
Rye - Malt	1.035
Sugar – Sucrose	1.046
Wheat – Flaked	1.035
Wheat – Malt	1.038
Wheat – Red	1.029
Wheat – White	1.030
Wheat – White malt	1.040

Fruit Juice - Brix, Specific Gravity

FRUIT	BRIX	SPECIFIC GRAVITY
Apple	4-6 (12)	1.045
Apricot	4-11 (9)	1.035
Blackberry	5-10 (6.5)	1.026
Blueberry	5-12 (7)	1.033
Cherry	9-19 (15)	1.064
Cranberry	3-5 (4)	1.024
Elderberry	7-11 (6)	1.030-1.046
Grape	15-25 (16)	1.065
Guava	7-11 (9)	1.036
Lime	0-14 (1)	1.000-1.010 (1.001)
Loganberry	(9)	1.035
Mango	11-21 (17)	1.045-1.09 (1.073)
Nectarine	6-12 (9)	1.022-1.047 (1.035)
Orange	2-7(11)	1.050
Papaya	8	1.031
Peach	6-12 (9)	1.022-1.047 (1.035)
Pear	7-13 (10)	1.026-1.052 (1.039)
Pineapple	13	1.052
Plum	11	1.043
Raspberry	7	1.026
Strawberry	3-10 (7)	1.013-1.043 (1.028)
Watermelon	9	1.040

Sugar Required for Target SG and PA

SPECIFIC GRAVITY (SG)	POTENTIAL ALCOHOL (PA%)	AMOUNT OF SUGAR/GAL WASH
1.010	1.3	2 oz.
1.015	1.9	4 oz.
1.020	2.6	7 oz.
1.025	3.3	9 oz.
1.030	3.9	12 oz.
1.035	4.6	15 oz.
1.040	5.2	17 oz.
1.045	5.9	19 oz.
1.050	6.6	21 oz.
1.055	7.2	23 oz.
1.060	7.9	25 oz.
1.065	8.5	27 oz.
1.070	9.2	29 oz.
1.075	9.9	31 oz.
1.080	10.5	33 oz.
1.085	11.2	36 oz.
1.090	11.8	38 oz.
1.095	12.5	40 oz.
1.100	13.2	42 oz.
1.105	13.8	44 oz.
1.110	14.5	46 oz.
1.115	15.1	48 oz.
1.120	15.8	50 oz.
1.125	16.5	52 oz.
1.130	17.1	54 oz.

From the Author

Greetings fellow distillers. Just a short bio about my background. I grew up in the hills of North Clark County in Washington State. I earned a Bachelor of Science Degree in Agriculture and a Bachelor of Arts Degree in Economics from Washington State University, Pullman, WA. I also have a Masters Degree in Technical Education from City University, Seattle, WA. After college I taught High School Agriculture Science, Agribusiness, Animal Science, Agricultural Biology and Horticulture for 32 years. I learned the distilling process at a licensed craft distillery in Washington State and have over 10 years of successful distilling experience. I have conducted countless hours of my own distilling research in my quest to perfect the home distilling process. As a technical educator I developed the ability to write instructional materials that are clear, concise, and affective in meeting the goal of teaching people how to do things; in this case, creating top-shelf spirits. I currently live with my wife Sandra in Cowlitz County, Washington State, a rural county where the art of distilling is highly appreciated.

Made in the USA
Las Vegas, NV
27 August 2024

94497597R00083